WebPlus X5 User Guide

How to Contact Us

Our main office
(UK, Europe):

The Software Centre
PO Box 2000, Nottingham,
NG11 7GW, UK

Main:	(0115) 914 2000
Registration (UK only):	(0800) 376 1989
Sales (UK only):	(0800) 376 7070
Customer Service/ Technical Support:	http://www.support.serif.com/
General Fax:	(0115) 914 2020

North American office
(USA, Canada):

Serif Inc, The Software Center,
17 Hampshire Drive, Suites 1 & 2,
Hudson, NH 03051, USA

Main:	(603) 889-8650
Registration:	(800) 794-6876
Sales:	(800) 55-SERIF or 557-3743
Customer Service/ Technical Support:	http://www.support.serif.com/
General Fax:	(603) 889-1127

Online

Visit us on the web at: http://www.serif.com/

International

Please contact your local distributor/dealer. For further details, please contact us at one of our phone numbers above.

This User Guide, and the software described in it, is furnished under an end user License Agreement, which is included with the product. The agreement specifies the permitted and prohibited uses.

Trademarks

Serif is a registered trademark of Serif (Europe) Ltd.

WebPlus is a registered trademark of Serif (Europe) Ltd.

All Serif product names are trademarks of Serif (Europe) Ltd.

Microsoft, Windows, and the Windows logo are registered trademarks of Microsoft Corporation. All other trademarks acknowledged.

Windows Vista and the Windows Vista Start button are trademarks or registered trademarks of Microsoft Corporation in the United States and/or other countries.

Copyrights

Contents

Contents

1 Welcome

Welcome!

Welcome to WebPlus X5 from **Serif**—the easiest way to get your business, organization, or household on the web!

To make life so much easier, WebPlus comes with an impressive selection of **design templates**, page **navigation bars**, creative **gallery** content, and **styles** for you to use. As a result, publishing to the web to a professional standard is easily achievable for experienced and inexperienced users alike! You'll also be able to reuse existing textual content by importing word processing documents.

To make the most of pictures in your site you can use **Image Cutout Studio** for cutting pictures out and **PhotoLab** for powerful image adjustment and effect combinations. You simply cannot afford to miss them!

WebPlus X5 doesn't just stop at "static" web publishing. The real power comes when adding and managing dynamic content, such as **blogs**, **forums**, **Content Management Systems (CMS)**, **counters**, and more. You can even make use of **E-commerce tools** for money-making shopping cart functionality.

Once you're happy with your WebPlus site, simply publish to the web to share with business colleagues, customers, friends and family alike.

Serif offers a range of competitively priced web hosting packages, allowing no-fuss publishing! For more details, visit the Serif Web Hosting (http://go.serif.com/hosting).

For a more detailed summary of what WebPlus can offer, see **Key features** (p. 4).

Upgrading?

If you've upgraded from a previous version, this new edition of WebPlus includes a host of **exciting new features** (p. 12) which keeps WebPlus ahead of its competitors and at a fraction of the price! We hope you also enjoy the additional power and performance edge.

Registration

Don't forget to register your new copy, using the **Registration Wizard**, on the **Help** menu. That way, we can keep you informed of new developments and future upgrades!

Key features

Before you get started with WebPlus, we recommend you take the opportunity to familiarize yourself with WebPlus key features and capabilities.

Layout

- **Theme Layout Design Templates**
  Choose a **theme** such as Arctic or Natural on which to base your site! Each theme offers a choice of commonly used page types—choose from About Us, Gallery, Products, and Contact pages, and many more. Pick **multiple layouts** as your new pages, then simply fill picture placeholders with your **own** pictures.

- **Ready-to-go Design Templates**
  Make "tailored" websites based on a chosen look and colour scheme in an instant. All **Pro design templates** are packed with **royalty-free** images for you to use.

- **Professional Layout Tools**
  Movable **rulers**, **guide lines** and a **dot grid**, as layout aids, help you position objects precisely; snapping jumps an object to guide or grid. Use **Sticky guides**, a great way of moving (in bulk) all objects snapped to your guide lines—move the guide and objects will follow! Instead, align and resize objects using **dynamic guide snapping**, without the need for ruler guides or precise object transforms.

- **Page Control**
  Add and **remove pages** in just a few clicks of your mouse in the **Site tab**. Drag and drop pages within the tab to reorder sequence. Assign **master pages** to several site pages at once for time saving and greater design consistency—even assign **multiple master pages** to a specific web page for more varied page design.

Website Essentials

- **QuickBuilder Bar for Easy Web Design**
  The simple way to get started with WebPlus—drag pages, navigation bars, text frames, images, Flash content, photo galleries, buttons, or Smart objects directly onto the page for quick results with no prior knowledge of the user interface.

- **Easy Site Structure**
  The hierarchical **Site tab** makes it easy to see the overall layout of your site.

- **Navigation Bars**
  Use intelligent **navigation bars** for site-wide page navigation—all bars update automatically to include any new pages you add, and can adopt many different design styles. You can also include forum, blog, and CMS articles in dynamically changing navigation bar submenus.

- **Site Search Tool**
  Perform **text searches** throughout the entire site with the powerful **Site Search Tool**.

- **Search Engine Optimization**
  Control how search engines index your website! Include or exclude pages from indexing by using search engine sitemap or robot files—protect confidentiality while offering potential web visitors accurate search results from your site.

- **Smart Objects**
  Serif Web Resources, Serif's Smart object hosting service, offers a series of interactive site features:

  - **Active Viewers**—shows many people are currently viewing a web page.

  - **Blogs**—add personal **profiles**, **social bookmarking links** and use **trackbacks** for inter-blog cross-referencing. Change blog appearance with different pre-defined **Visual Styles** (or use your own!) Use **Editor groups** for multi-author article publishing.

  - **Content Management System (CMS)**—this allows content providers to add and update web content from anywhere, without WebPlus and without the need to re-publish your site.

- **Forum**—stimulates lively thread-based discussions in a full-sized window. Create multiple forums and manage independently (moderate discussions and set up user login access).

- **Hit Counters**—adds a counter showing the number of hits on the current page.

- **News**—for simple news announcements such as website updates or next club meeting dates.

- **Poll**—adds an online poll to canvass web visitor's opinions.

- **Resource booking**—Use calendar-based **Resource booking** to self-manage bookings for accommodation, conference and meeting facilities, squash courts, and more.

- **Shout Box**—Adds an interactive chat window to your web page.

- **User List**—offers page or site access control by management of "zonal" **user groups** (e.g., Personnel). Web visitors can self-register via a site's user login (with optional email activation).

- **Active Document Frames**
  Hyperlinks can open a page in a document frame on another page. Set an **Absolute URL** for more accurate inter-frame navigation.

- **Google Maps**
  Embed a Google Map directly into your "Directions" web page. Add your own **multiple markers** to pinpoint locations such as offices, depots, places of interest, and events.

- **Generate Revenue with Google AdSense**
  Add Google-driven advertising space on your website, while Google pays you... 24/7!

- **Site Management Tools**
  Manage all your **Page/Master Page Properties**, **resources**, **fonts**, **text**, **hyperlinks**, and **anchors**—all from within WebPlus's **Site Manager**. Powerfully manage web pages individually, by selection, or apply to all pages. Site Checker detects Site Navigation, Text Formatting, and Form/e-commerce problems and carries out automatic fixes where possible.

- **Track Site Usage Anywhere**
  Sign up to **Google Analytics** for comprehensive tracking and monitoring of your website's visitor data. Analyse data online at any time with easy-to-interpret charts and maps.

Pictures

- **Import Pictures**
  Import commonly-used standard file formats, including all the latest RAW digital camera formats, Photoshop files, HD photos, and Serif metafiles (for sharing graphics between Serif applications). Import multiple images and paste one by one!

- **Picture Power with Media Bar**
  No more repetitive photo importing! Keep photo content to hand in the **Media Bar**—drag and drop from the Media Bar onto pictures to replace! Search for pictures by their metadata. Control picture sizing and alignment within its frame.

- **Stunning Online Photo Galleries!**
  Wow your friends, family and colleagues with stunning SlideShowPro™ (Flash), Flash, and JavaScript photo galleries. Various gallery styles offer photo navigation by selection from thumbnails, thumbnail rollovers, photo grid or photo stack. Take advantage of caption support (using EXIF data), and create and manage albums.

- **Quick-and-easy Image Cutouts**
  Image Cutout Studio makes light work of cutting out your placed pictures, directly in WebPlus. Use brushes to discard uniform backgrounds (sky, walls, etc.) or keep subjects of interest (people, objects, etc.).

- **Image Adjustments**
  Apply **adjustments** (Brightness, Contrast, fix red eye, and more) or use **Edit in PhotoPlus**, which accesses Serif's award-winning photo-editing package (if installed).

- **PhotoLab for Non-destructive Adjustment and Effect Filters**
  The powerful **PhotoLab** packs a punch with an impressive selection of editable adjustments, creative, and artistic effects (pencil, water colour, oil, and more). Use integrated **Straighten**, **Crop**, **Red-eye**, and **Spot-repair** tools for easy **retouching**. Apply filters to selected areas

of your photo by using **brush-based masking**. **Save** adjustment/effect combinations as favourites for future use.

- **A Versatile Metafile Format**
  Import and Export Serif Metafiles (SMF), a proprietary image format with improvements to the Windows Metafile format (WMF). Better line, fill, and text definitions make them ideal for sharing graphics between Serif applications.

- **Pop-up Rollovers**
  Create your own simple photo gallery—show a larger version of a picture on thumbnail hover over.

- **Decorative Picture Frames**
  Exciting ready-to-go **picture frames** can be applied directly to pictures straight from the Gallery tab.

Media

- **YouTube® Videos**
  Pick your favourite YouTube® videos and include them on your web page!

- **Podcasts**
  Create your own **podcast** feeds and broadcast your own audio and video episodes frequently and easily. Web visitors can subscribe with all the most popular web browsers and via on-click subscription to Google Reader®, My Yahoo!®, and Apple iTunes®.

Creative

- **Drawing Tools**
  Design stunning vector graphics with Pencil, Pen and Straight **Line tools**, and add line endings like arrowheads, diamonds, and quills. Alternatively, the array of fully-customizable **QuickShapes** let you quickly create outlines for your designs, while **Convert to Curves**, **Crop to Shape**, and curve drawing offer complete flexibility for creating any shape imaginable! **Mesh warp envelopes** add perspective, slant, and bulge to any object.

- **Ready-to-use Styles**
  Choose various filter effects, glows, shadows, textures, and materials
  from the Styles tab. Customize the preset styles or store your own!

- **Transparency**
  Add transparency to your backgrounds, text frames, tables, shapes and
  text to achieve a truly professional look. As with colour fills, you can
  apply **solid**, **gradient**, and **bitmap** transparencies—even create bitmap
  transparencies from your own image collection.

- **Intelligent Colour Schemes**
  Use the **Colour Scheme Designer** to swap the colours used in your
  website—all via a single click! Either use scheme presets or design
  your very own **custom colour schemes** using spreads based on
  accepted colour theory.

- **New 2D/3D Filter Effects**
  Add stunning **reflections** of an object—great for web page titles and
  pictures! **Blur** any object or stroke a coloured solid or gradient border
  around object edges (stroke with a new **Contour** fill which applies
  gradient fill from the inner to outer outline width). 3D effects are
  boosted with realistic glass-like **Transparency** control of non-
  reflective/reflective surfaces and multiple separately coloured lights
  for dramatic lighting effects. All filter effects can be applied in
  preview mode or to the object on the page. Use the new **Shadow Tool**
  for on-the-page shadow control.

- **Instant 3D with On-screen Transforms**
  Transform 3D objects **in-situ** with 3D editing from a context toolbar.
  Apply multi-coloured **lighting effects** (with directional control), along
  with custom **bevel** and **lathe** effect profiles to create your very own
  unique contours. **Hardware-accelerated rendering** boosts redraw
  performance (hardware dependent).

Text

- **Import Word and Open Office text documents**
  Add word processing content to any text frame without fuss! Import
  doesn't need the application to be installed locally! Use a choice of
  import converters to optimize text import.

- **Artistic and frame text**
  Have complete control over your text with WebPlus's DTP-style text control. Artistic text can be used to give your websites high impact—especially good for titling or adding to a drawn path. HTML text frames allow you to remain HTML compliant with AutoFit or manual text fitting. All text has editing capabilities compatible with top of the range word processors!

- **Text Frames**
  Compose story text in **text frames** then easily position or size the frame to suit. Separate crop and wrap outlines mean you have greater control over where text flows and how it appears. Import, paste, export text in **Unicode** format... design with a foreign-language or special fonts and characters. Text paths also benefit from intelligent text fitting.

- **Fonts**
  Substitute missing fonts when opening third-party projects. View your currently installed font set in the Fonts tab, including those most recently assigned to text, favourite fonts, and those considered Websafe. Hover over a listed font for an "in-situ" **font preview** of your selected text—simply click to apply the new font if you like it! Easily **swap** all selected instances of a common font for another font in one fell swoop!

- **Attach and position shapes and pictures to text**
  Control the positioning of **shapes** and **pictures** within your HTML or Creative text frames (or in relation to artistic text titles).

- **Tables and Calendars**
  Choose from a range of preset formats or design your own **custom** table or calendar. Use the convenient Table context toolbar to sort data, format cells, and choose from a wide range of functions for **spreadsheet calculations** (use absolute cell references). **Calendars** are table-based for enhanced functionality, and support Year update, inline personal events, and public holidays!

- **Find & Replace**
  Search through story text for words and phrases but also text attributes, particular fonts, colours, special characters (Unicode), regular expressions, and words at specific positions in sentences.

- **Database Merge**
  Present database content on your web page from Serif databases
  (.SDB), Microsoft Access (.MDB), dBASE, ODBC server data, and
  other well known database formats, as well as Microsoft Excel,
  HTML, and delimited text files. Product lists, mailing lists,
  inventories, in fact any database information can be served to your
  web audience. Place text or pictures into **repeating areas**, repeating
  Buy Now or **Add to Shopping Cart e-commerce forms**, or even
  HTML fragments. Create your own **photo database** (with EXIF
  fields) for subsequent merging.

Web Publishing

- **Previewing your work**
  Test drive your new web page or your entire site in a choice of
  different installed web browsers.

- **Publish your site**
  Publish to a local folder or upload directly to your ISP via FTP;
  upload any new or edited pages incrementally. Use **Quick Publish** to
  upload and view a currently displayed page—great for live verification
  of individual pages as you build your website.

New features

- **Button Studio** (see p. 83)
  Make your own **custom buttons** for your navigation bars in Button Studio, an environment tailor made for **focused button design**. All the key WebPlus tools are at hand for **editing in each button state** (e.g., Normal, Down, Hover), along with intelligent **button scaling control**. You can also use buttons as standalone objects, or even convert to a navigation bar in one click!

- **New Navigation Bars** (see p. 67)
  Take time out to explore exciting new intelligent navigation bars, ranging in type from **Block**, **Graphic**, **Speech**, and **Tab**, to **Standard** and **Traditional**. Buttons, separators, and background presets for the bar and pop-up menus can be **customized** or **created from scratch** in the new Button Studio and Design Studio, giving you absolute design control.

- **Pop-up Menus** (see p. 78)
  Using the site structure (or custom), create a **pop-up navigation menu** that displays from any WebPlus object (button, Gallery object, QuickShape, or picture).

- **Panels** (see p. 106)
  Create **panels** as containers for **displaying extra details**, **helpful tips**, **shortcuts**, **converted navigation bars**, **PayPal Buy Now Forms**.. in fact any objects you like. Optionally **float** panels that stay locked to your browser window for permanent display (even when page scrolling). With **actions** you can connect a **hidden panel** to any object to display on rollover or mouse-click of that object (great for buttons, Gallery objects, pictures). Also use actions for pop-up **alert messages** or **initiate printing** via buttons placed on your page.

- **PayPal® Mini Carts!** (see p. 150)
  Set up a floating E-commerce shopping cart window that pops up as items are added, then minimizes to be always "at hand". Great for keeping a track on purchases!

- **Enhanced Google Maps** (see p. 97)
  Pinpoint exact "photo" locations using **Google Street View**, directly off any clicked map marker. Google Maps now support an unlimited number of map markers!

Ease of Use

- **Hover-based indication of Selection** (see p. 227)
  For use in more complex multi-object web page designs, objects "glow" on hover over to indicate selection.

- **Lasso Selection** (see p. 228)
  The **Lasso Tool** selects specific objects in complicated designs more easily. Simply drag around the "target" object to include in selection.

- **Independent Master Page Objects** (see p. 48)
  For more design freedom, **promote master page objects** to your page, making them detached and available for independent editing. As a visual aid, master page objects can now be distinguished from page objects by different bounding box colour; objects from different master pages can also be distinguished from each other!

- **Business User Details per Site!** (see p. 212)
  Create groupings of business user details, called **Business Sets**; apply a business set to each site. Ideal for WebPlus web developers looking for design flexibility across multiple sites.

- **User-defined Variables** (see p. 215)
  Set up your own **variables** to automatically update common terms that repeat throughout your website. Great for updating product names, prices, product versions, and language variants all at the same time.

- **At-a-glance Objects per Page**
  Great for listing objects on your page/master page/pasteboard, the **Objects tab** allows object location, reorder, and master page attachment in complex page designs.

Creative

- **Gradient and Bitmap Fills and Transparency on Outlines** (see p. 328)
  Get even more creative with your object outlines! Apply **linear**, **elliptical**, **conical**, and **bitmap** fills and transparency around shapes and text frames for eye-catching design.

- **Exciting and modern colour schemes** (see p. 321)
  Experiment with an impressive selection of mood-inducing **schemes**,
  each capable of transforming your site's "look and feel" in one click.
  Ideal for updating sites based on theme layout design templates. The
  Colour Scheme Designer also now hosts a **Colour Picker** to allow
  your custom scheme to be based on any picked workspace colour.

Pictures

- **Pictures via Lightboxes** (see p. 103)
  Click picture thumbnails to present maximized pictures in a **pop-up
  lightbox**—also perfect for floating login boxes, forms, web pages to
  save valuable space. All lightboxes float over your page to stunning
  effect, with an optional slideshow feature, captioning, and styling!

- **Import Scalable Vector Graphics** (see p. 256)
  Add logos, buttons, and other vector art to your page using the modern
  browser-friendly SVG format (including compressed SVG).

- **Import Microsoft Word 2010 documents** (see p. 187)
  Just as for Word 2007 documents you can now import Word 2010
  documents directly into text frames!

- **Import Custom User Settings on Upgrade**
  Upgrading from WebPlus X4? Now preserve your **custom Gallery
  content**, **object styles**, **preferences**, **user dictionaries**, keyboard
  shortcuts, **PDF profiles**, and much more—all from within WebPlus
  X5.

> WebPlus Help lists additional minor product improvements on
> previous versions. See the New Features topic in Help for more
> details.

Installation

System Requirements

Minimum:

- Windows-based PC with DVD drive and mouse

- Microsoft Windows® XP (32 bit), Windows® Vista, or Windows® 7 operating system

- 512MB RAM

- 336MB free hard disk space

- 1024 x 768 monitor resolution

- Internet Explorer 5.5 (6.0 or above for Smart object use)

Additional disk resources and memory are required when editing large and/or complex sites.

Optional:

- Windows-compatible printer

- TWAIN-compatible scanner and/or digital camera

- 3D Accelerated graphics card with DirectX 9 (or above) or OpenGL support

- .NET 2.0 for text import filters (Word 2007/2010 + OpenOffice) (installed by default)

- Internet account and connection required for Publishing to web and accessing online resources

First-time install

To install WebPlus, simply insert the WebPlus X5 Program DVD into your DVD drive. The AutoRun feature automatically starts the Setup process. Just answer the on-screen questions to install the program.

Re-install

To re-install the software or to change the installation at a later date, select **Settings/Control Panel** from the Windows Start menu and then click on the **Add/Remove Programs** icon. Make sure the WebPlus X5 Program DVD is inserted into your DVD drive, click the **Install...** button and then simply follow the on-screen instructions.

2 Getting Started

Startup Wizard

On program launch, the Startup Wizard is displayed which offers different routes into WebPlus:

The options are self explanatory, where site creation can be made from scratch or from a pre-supplied design template. Previously saved sites can be opened or non-WebPlus web pages can be imported into your site from file or URL.

- **Start New Site**, to create your own site from scratch.

- **Use Design Template**, to create an instant site from a pre-designed template.

- **Get More**, to access a range of free resources and design templates (purchasable).

- **WebPlus hosting**, to host your published WebPlus site with Serif.

- **Open**, to access recently opened sites. Hover over each entry for a quick preview!

- **Learn** area, to access tutorials, support information, and more.

Use the **Choose Workspace** drop-down menu to choose your workspace appearance (i.e., Studio tab positions, tab sizes, and show/hide tab status). You can adopt the default workspace profile **<Default Profile>**, the last used profile **<Current Profile>**, a range of profile presets, or a workspace profile you have previously saved.

> As you click on different profiles from the menu, your workspace will preview each tab layout in turn.

The Startup Wizard is displayed by default when you launch WebPlus. You can switch it off via the **Don't show this wizard again** option on the Startup Wizard screen, or on again via the **Use Startup Wizard** check box in **Tools>Options...** (use Options>General menu option).

Creating a site using a design template

WebPlus comes complete with a whole range of categorized design templates which will speed you through the creation of all kinds of websites.

Each template offers:

- **Complementary design**—Professionally designed layout with high-visual impact.

- **Schemes**—choose a named colour scheme to apply a specific look and feel.

- **Page selection**—select some or all template pages (e.g., Home, Products, About Us, etc.) to base your new site on.

Design templates come in two types—**theme layouts**, where you pick your own pictures, or **ready-to-go Pro templates** which are already populated with pictures.

Theme layouts

These offer a choice of themes (e.g., Doodle) on which to base your site; you'll get picture placeholders instead of actual pictures. Simply add your own pictures to placeholders and personalize placeholder text, then publish.

Ready-to-go Pro templates

These are categorized templates containing royalty-free pictures which can be adopted to fast-track you to your completed website. You just need to personalize placeholder text, then publish.

To create a site using a design template:

1. Launch WebPlus, or choose **Startup Wizard...** from the **File** menu, to display the Startup Wizard.

2. Select **Use Design Template**.

3. From the dialog, select a Theme Layout or Pro template design from the main pane.

Theme Layouts

Pro Design Templates

Pro templates are grouped into subject-based categories; use the scroll bar or collapse a category to reveal more options (click the ⊟ button next to the category name). The right-hand pane refreshes to display thumbnails of that template's available pages.

✓ Home

4. From the right-hand pane, decide which pages you wish to be part of your site. Check or uncheck under each page to select, or click **Select All** to select all pages (click **Deselect All** to clear the current selection).

About Us

5. Pick a **Colour Scheme** from the drop-down list at the top of the dialog (the first three schemes are designed specifically for the chosen template). The page thumbnails refresh to reflect the new page's appearance. For a closer look, use the Zoom In/Zoom Out buttons or Zoom slider at the bottom of the dialog.

✓ Gallery

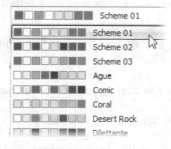

6. Click **Open**.

The site opens to the first (Home) page, with the Studio's Site tab displayed on the right, showing the various pages that comprise the site in its Site Structure tree.

💡 Template categories, apart from WebPlus X5 Pro Templates, let you access additional purchasable templates from Serif.

🔍 As each template is colour schemed, you can swap the underlying scheme to change the site's colours at any time!

⚲ You can save any WebPlus site as a template (*.wpx) file to be used as a basis for other sites. See Saving your own templates in WebPlus Help.

Starting a site from scratch

Although design templates can simplify your design choices, you can just as easily start out from scratch with a new, blank site.

To start a new site from scratch using the Startup Wizard:

- Launch WebPlus.
  - or -

  Click 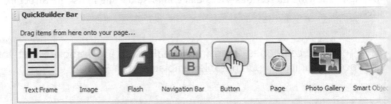 **New Site** from the **Standard** toolbar.

- Select **Create>Start New Site**.

The new site opens with a blank page using default page properties.

🖋 If you click ❌ **Cancel** from the Startup Wizard, you'll get the same result.

To start a new site during your WebPlus session:

- Choose **New** from the **File** menu.

To help you quickly build a site from scratch, WebPlus offers the **QuickBuilder Bar**. The tab hosts commonly used objects and features which can be introduced onto your web page by drag-and-drop, avoiding the need to initially understand the range of WebPlus toolbars.

Opening an existing site

You can open an existing WebPlus site from the Startup Wizard, via the **Standard** toolbar, or via the **File** menu. It is also possible to Import web pages from existing HTML websites via the **File** menu. (See online help or more details.)

To open an existing WebPlus site (Startup Wizard):

Open

RealEstate22.wpp

PaintTheWorld.wpp

XR Finance.wpp

holiday_site.

design65.wp

fred.wpp

Finance

XR Finance.wpp

1. From the Startup Wizard, review your sites from the Open section. The most recently opened site will be shown at the top of the list. To see a thumbnail preview of any site before opening, hover over its name in the list.

2. Click the file name to open it.

> If your site hasn't been opened recently, click ☐ **Browse...** to navigate to it.

To open existing WebPlus sites (during WebPlus session):

1. Click 📂 **Open** on the **Standard** toolbar.

2. In the **Open** dialog, select the folder and file name(s). For multiple sites, **Shift**-click to select adjacent multiple files or **Ctrl**-click to select non-adjacent files.

3. Click the **Open** button.

To open sites by drag-and-drop:

- From Windows Explorer, drag and drop the site's preview thumbnail anywhere onto the WebPlus workspace.

To revert to the saved version of an open site:

- Choose **Revert** from the **File** menu.

Font substitution

WebPlus supports automatic font substitution as you open a WebPlus site which has fonts which are not stored on your computer. The dialog that shows also lets you manually substitute a missing font if necessary. See online Help for more details.

Working with more than one site

If you have multiple websites open at the same time it's easy to jump between them using different methods.

w456.wpp *

Click on a Window tab at the top of the workspace to make it active (e.g., w456.wpp).

1 w123.wpp

✓ 2 w456.wpp *

3 w789.wpp

Alternatively, you can select the name of a currently open site from the **Window** menu. Unsaved websites are indicated by an asterisk; the currently active site is shown with a tick. In the example opposite, the w456.wpp site is active and also unsaved.

Saving your site

To save your work:

- Click 📅 **Save** on the **Standard** toolbar.

- To save under a different name, choose **Save As...** from the **File** menu.

✎ An unsaved site will have an asterisk after its name shown in either its Window tab or on the **Window** menu.

3 Setting up Sites and Pages

Understanding site structure and navigation

Unlike a printed publication, a website doesn't depend on a linear page sequence. When designing a site, it makes more sense to think of the site in spatial terms, with a **structure** like that of a museum which people will explore. You can generally assume that your visitors will come in through the "front door" (the Home page)—but where they go after that depends on the links you've provided. These **navigation** pathways are like corridors that connect the various rooms of the museum. It's up to you as the "architect" to develop a sensible arrangement of pages and links so that visitors can find their way around easily, without getting lost.

In WebPlus, you can use the **Site Structure tree** to visually map out the structure of your site and then add navigation bars—that dynamically adapt to the structure you've defined.

Site structure

Unlike the museum in our analogy, the "structure" of a website has nothing to do with its physical layout, or where pages are stored. Rather, it's a way of logically arranging the content on the site so that visitors have an easier time navigating through it. One of the most useful organizing principles—which WebPlus strongly reinforces—is an "inverted tree" structure that starts with the Home page and then branches out to other pages. To the visitor navigating your site, this arrangement presents your content in a familiar, hierarchical way, structured into **sections** and **levels**.

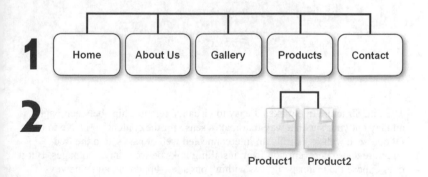

- A **section** is a content category, for example "Gallery", "Products", or "Contact". The various major sections are typically listed on the site's Home page in a navigation bar. Ideally, each page on the site belongs to a particular section. And unless there's only one page in a given section, the section will have its own main page, which usually serves as a menu for subsidiary pages.

- The **level** is the number of steps (i.e., jumps) a given page is removed from the Home page. The Home page will always reside at Level 1, normally along with main section menu pages. This allows navigation bars to work easily and automatically. Pages one step "below" the section menu pages reside at Level 2, and are considered to be "**child**" pages of the "**parent**" page. For example, a parent Products page could have two child pages called Product1 and Product2.

In WebPlus, the Site Structure tree (in the **Site tab**) provides a visual aid that lets you organize the content on your site into sections and levels. Here's how the same structure might appear in the WebPlus Site Structure tree:

The Site Structure tree makes it easy to visualize relationships between pages and lay out your site in a way that makes sense for the content you have to offer. Of course, a website is truly an interconnected web of pages, and the tree structure doesn't prevent you from installing links between any two pages. But it does expose the major pathways within your site—up, down, and sideways. Logical section/level design makes your site easier to navigate, and WebPlus makes it simple to create **navigation bars** that mirror your site structure and help guide your visitors along those "main roads."

Incidentally, WebPlus also supports **HTML pages** and **offsite links** which can be inserted into the Site Structure as for any other page. Page icons for both are slightly different in design to a standard web page to indicate that it is based only on HTML code (See p. 52) or that it points to a location outside of the website. As an example, compare the HTML page "Overview," the standard web page "Sales," and the offsite link "Member's forum."

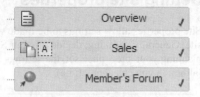

Navigation

In WebPlus, adding navigation between your web pages is easy with navigation bars, each pre-programmed to understand your site structure, making it easy to design a site that's simple to navigate. You simply select one from the Web Objects toolbar and WebPlus does the rest!

For example, here's a navigation bar we selected for the site shown in the main tree above. The buttons provide links to the Home and section menu pages (all at Level 1) and pop-up menus that link to child pages (Level 2 in this case).

For more information, see Adding navigation bars on p. 67.

Setting site properties

Site properties allow settings to be made which will be applied across the entire site. Generally speaking, decide on your Site property settings when you are planning your site—once set, the settings do not normally need to be modified (although you can at any time).

Some site properties such as page appearance and search-engine optimization settings are also mirrored on individual pages (via Page Properties; see p. 56). This lets you override or complement the "global" Site Properties, respectively, and apply "local" settings to specific pages.

To view or change site property settings:

- Choose **Site Properties...** from the **File** menu. The Site Properties dialog appears, with each displayed menu option reflecting an aspect of site properties.

Menu Option	Property
Page (default)	**Default page alignment** Lets you set a default horizontal page alignment (Left or Centred). **Default page size** Default Width and Height settings determine the dimensions of new standard web pages or master pages. **Page Appearance** Sets the site-wide schemed or non-schemed colours for hyperlinks, on-page colour, and background colour.
File Naming	**Default page file extension** The default extension for published pages is .HTML. Some web servers require you to use a different extension. **Warn about upper case characters in filenames** When creating new pages, the user will be warned if upper case characters are used when creating the page's file name.

Resource File Names
Controls the formatting of resource file names to allow
successful upload to ISPs which impose file naming
constraints.

Publishing **Site URL**
Defines the full URL address. This is a requirement for search
engine optimization with sitemaps or RSS feeds.

FTP account
Sets the default FTP account used for web publishing.

FTP account settings
Displays the default FTP account settings.

Graphics **Global image export options**
Applies default format, resampling, naming, optimization, and
linking settings when exporting graphics.

HTML **HTML Output and Default HTML IDs**
Output Control how your web pages are output by choosing from
different encoding methods and controlling which HTML IDs
are generated.

Page header
Add author details and copyright details to your site's page
headers.

Features **Smart Objects**
Overrides your Blog, Forum, or CMS colours with selectable
non-schemed colours or your site's current schemed colours.

Features **Smart Objects**
Applies the current site's colour scheme to Smart Objects such
as blogs, forums, and CMS.

Lightbox **General Settings**
Sets the site-wide settings for lightboxes. Border, border
colour, content colour/opacity, and play settings can be
configured.

Caption Settings
Sets the caption font, position, size, font colour/opacity, and
text background colour.

Background Settings
Sets the background colour/opacity.

Lightbox Preview
Click **Preview Lightbox...** to test the lightbox settings you've just made.

Favourites Icon	**Show a favourites icon..** Set an icon file (a graphic) for the site which will show when a web visitor bookmarks your website.
Search	**Search engine descriptors** Include optional descriptive information and keywords for your site.
Search Engine	**Sitemaps and robots** Informs search engines or robots if they can crawl, analyze and index web pages in your site. A Sitemap file will include web pages to be indexed whereas a Robots meta tag (or a robots.txt file) controls which pages are to be excluded from indexing.
Summary	**Properties and statistics** View and change information for the current site.

Setting page size and alignment

Default site property settings for **Width** and **Height** determine the dimensions of any new page or master page. A default site property setting for **alignment** (either Left or Centred) determines how page content lines up in a browser.

One of the first things you may want to do, when creating a new site from scratch, is to check the default dimensions and adjust them if necessary. You can adjust the dimension settings at any time—but as a rule, make changes before you've gone too far with laying out page elements!

In general, use a page **Width** setting that will fit on a standard monitor (750 pixels is usually safe) and won't force users to scroll horizontally.

For page dimension and alignment, you can override the site setting for a particular page, as described in Setting page properties on p. 56.

To set the site-wide page dimension settings:

- From the dialog's **Page** menu option, select different **Width** and/or **Height** values to apply to pages.

You can also change the default page alignment setting as a site property.

To set the site-wide page alignment setting:

- From the dialog's **Page** menu option, select either "Left" or "Centred" in the **Default page alignment** drop-down menu.

Setting page appearance

Hyperlink colour, on-page colour, background colour, and your background image can be controlled globally via site properties. This means all you created web pages will adopt these settings, although you have the option to override on-page and background settings per page. See Setting page properties on p. 56.

By default, sites based on a template or those created from scratch use schemed colours for their hyperlink and on-page colours. These colours belong to the site's current colour scheme but you can swap to a different scheme or change the individual colours at any time. See Using colour schemes on p. 321.

To set hyperlink, on-page and background colours:

1. From the dialog's **Page** menu option, in the Page Appearance section, click the down arrow for the colour you want to change.

2. Select a different colour from the drop-down list, which shows numbered scheme colours and other colours. Select **More Colour...** to optionally pick from a Colour Selector dialog.

3. Click **OK**.

To set a background picture:

1. Under the Page Appearance section, click **Background Image...**.

2. Check **Use Background Image**, then locate and select the image from the Import Picture dialog. Click **Open**.

- Use **Export Options...** to decide if the image is to be converted on export or kept as is.

- When checked, **Scrolls with page** scrolls the image background independently of the page contents in the browser window; if unchecked the background cannot scroll with page content.

- The **Repeat** drop-down menu controls how your image is repeated on the background (Horizontal, Vertical, or Tiled). The option None places just a single image.

- The **Position** drop-down menu sets the position of your image (e.g., Top Centre). For repeating image backgrounds, the image is repeated from this initial position. You can also specify a **Custom...** position, which sets the image's position in relation to its top-left corner.

3. Click **OK**.

If you use an image background with transparent regions, the Background colour is still active and will show through; otherwise the picture will cover the background colour.

If you make the on-page colour transparent, the image background shows, making the page boundaries invisible (content is still constrained to page dimensions).

For more details on other tab settings, see online Help.

Search engine optimization

Indexing involves the automatic collection of information about your web pages by search engines such as Google, Yahoo, and many more. By "harvesting" this information at the search engine, search engine users can make use of this indexed information to obtain quick and accurate site search results which match the search criteria entered by the user.

By default, the contents of each published web page (especially heading text) will be indexed. However, in an Internet world of billions of web pages all being constantly indexed, web developers can optimize this indexing process to allow a site's pages to appear higher in a user's search results.

Optimization of web pages for search engines is possible in several ways:

- **Page Titling**: Page titles can be created in addition to page names. This allows search results to report your pages with a more useful title rather than just the page name. For example, in search results, an American birds home page could report "American Birds Home Page" instead of just "Home" followed by the page's description. See Setting page, title, and file names.

- **Description** and **Keywords** meta tags: For the site and/or individual pages, **descriptive text** can be added to the site/page which will be included in any matching search results associated with your site/page. **Keywords** allow better matching between entered search engine text (like you might enter into Google) and the keywords you've associated with your site or page. Additionally, a **robots meta tag** also lets you include/exclude the site or pages from being indexed; hyperlinks to other pages can also be prevented from being explored (crawled by "spiders").

- **Image ALT Text**: Alternative text, used instead of a image which can't be displayed, can be exploited by search engine robots. See Setting image export options.

- **Hyperlink Title text**: Supporting descriptive text (e.g., "See our new product range") shown when hovering over a hyperlink destination can also be exploited by search engine robots. See Adding hyperlinks and anchors.

- **Robots**: Pages (or folders) can be **excluded** from search-engine indexing by using a robots file. This works in an equivalent way to the robots meta tag but uses a text file (robots.txt) to instruct robots or spiders what **not** to index. The file simply lists excluded site page/folder references.

- **Sitemaps**: The opposite of the "robots" concept; pages can be **included** to aid and optimize intelligent crawling/indexing. site page references are stored in a dedicated sitemap file (sitemap.xml).

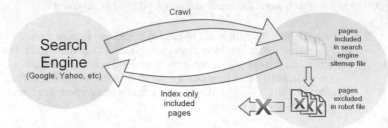

Whether you are using Meta tags, robots, or sitemaps independently or in combination, WebPlus makes configuration simple. As these settings can be established or modified for the whole site (Site Properties; Search Engine menu option) any newly created page will adopt site's search engine settings. If you change the site settings, all web pages will update to the new settings automatically. However, you can override the site's settings on a specific web page (Page Properties; Search Engine menu option) at any time. The page's override means that subsequent changes to site settings will always be ignored for those pages.

Using titles, descriptions and tags

Although they're optional, if you want to increase the likelihood that your website will be "noticed" by major web search services, you should optimize your page titles, and enter appropriate descriptions and tags. Search services maintain catalogues of web pages, often compiled through the use of "crawlers" or other programs that prowl the web collecting data on sites and their content. By including descriptive titles, descriptions and tags, you'll assist these engines in processing your site's information. You can enter titles, descriptions and tags for the site as a whole and/or for individual pages. For example, for a simple ornithological site:

	In Site Properties	In Page Properties
Title	N/A	American Birds: Egrets and Herons Gallery
Description	This unique photo gallery website showcases the beauty and diversity of North American birdlife.	These are larger bird species found in freshwater marshes, coastal lagoons, and even along seashores.
Keywords	Birds, America, Audubon	Cattle Egret, Blue Heron, Green-backed Heron

To enter search engine descriptors:

1. (For the site) Choose **Site Properties...** from the **File** menu.
   - or -
   (For a page) Right-click the page in the workspace (or Site tab) and choose **Page Properties...** (or choose the item from the **Edit** menu).

2. Click the dialog's **Search** menu option.

3. In the top window, type in a brief description of your site. Although the description can be any length, the first ten words or so are the most important.

4. In the next window, enter any number of keywords (separated by commas) that you think fairly categorize your site/page. Put yourself in the place of a potential visitor. What keywords might they enter if they were searching for exactly what your site or page has to offer?

5. Set a language code from the drop-down menu to identify the language use. Most user's Internet search engines will permit language specific searches for web pages, so your site will show in search results according to its language code setting.

Excluding pages from indexing (robots meta tags)

A robots meta tag can be used to control how search engine robots access the site or page. The whole site (and pages) can be set to be indexed/not indexed, page hyperlinks followed/not followed, or any combination thereof. Site-wide settings are made by checking **Index pages on this site** and **Follow links from pages** or as overrides on specific page properties.

To enable robot Meta Tag generation:

1. (For the site) Choose **Site Properties...** from the **File** menu.
   - or -
   (For a page) Right-click the page in the workspace or Site tab and choose **Page Properties...** (or choose the item from the **Edit** menu).

2. Select the Search Engine menu option and check the **Create robots meta tags** option (for a page you'll need to override site-wide settings).

3. (For the site) Use the two suboptions to allow or prevent search engines indexing the entire site (check/uncheck **Index pages on this site** option) or to allow or prevent indexing of all pages linked from an indexed page (check/uncheck **Follow links from pages** option).
    - or -
    (For the page) Ensure **Override site search engine settings** is checked, then check **Create robots meta tag** and check/uncheck the equivalent suboptions for the specific page.

Excluding pages from indexing (Robots file)

The objective of this method is the same as that for using a robots meta tag, but instead a robots.txt file is created and no robots meta tag is included in web pages. The robots.txt file is stored in the web site's root folder and can be viewed in any text editor to verify the excluded pages and folders.

To enable a robots.txt file:

1. Choose **Site Properties...** from the **File** menu.

2. From the Search Engine menu option, check **Create search engine robots file**.

3. (For the site) To allow or prevent search engines indexing the entire site (check/uncheck **Index pages on this site** option).
    - or -
    (For a page) From page properties, to prevent search engines indexing the page, ensure **Override site search engine settings** is checked, then uncheck the **Index this page** option.

Including pages in indexing

So far we've looked primarily at methods of excluding web pages from indexing. Without these controls, web pages will be indexed by discovering page hyperlinks and crawling through them, harvesting keywords, descriptions, and page text to be indexed. However, this process may not be efficient as there may be a limited number of inter-page hyperlinks present throughout your site. As a result, a search engine **sitemap file** (sitemap.xml) can be created to act as a local lookup for crawlers to begin investigating your site. The file simply lists pages in your site that you've decided can be indexed. The file also indicates to search engines when pages have been modified, informs when the search engine should check the page and how "important" pages are in relation to each other.

Just like the robots file, the setting of site and page properties creates the sitemap file (this is published with your site); the file is stored in the root web folder (perhaps alongside a robots.txt file).

> One requirement of using search engine sitemaps is the need to declare an absolute URL. This allows the proper URL address (e.g., www.helloworld.com) to be indexed, allowing search engine users to link through to your site from their search results.

To enable search engine sitemaps:

1. Choose **Site Properties...** from the **File** menu.

2. From the Search Engine menu option, check the **Create search engine sitemap file** option.

3. (Optional) When the above option is checked, the default sitemap.xml file can be renamed. Click the **Change...** button and edit accordingly.

4. (For the site) To populate the sitemap file with a list of all the site's web pages (for improved page "discovery"), the **Index pages on this site** option is checked. Uncheck to create an empty sitemap.xml file.
   - or -
   (For a page) From page properties, to add the page to the sitemap file, ensure **Override site search engine settings** and **Index this page** are checked. This assumes the site as a whole has not been listed in the sitemap.xml file.

5. Check/uncheck Sitemap settings including:

   - Page's last modified date and time.

   - Page change frequency (set drop-down menu to hourly, daily, weekly, monthly, yearly, or never): This suggests to the search engine how frequently the page is likely to change. The search engine will decide how often to index the page on the basis of this setting.

   - Page priority rating: 0.0 (lowest) to 1.0 (highest). Sets a page priority relative to your other web pages by which search engines are most likely to index. The default can be set on site properties with specific page overrides setting a priority higher or lower than the default.

Prioritizing text with Heading HTML tags

It is possible to assign paragraphs (or text styles) in your HTML frame or
HTML table with a preferred HTML tags (H1, H2, .., to H6) for export. The tags
can be assigned from **Paragraph...** on the **Text** menu (choose the
Paragraph>HTML option); simply pick a preferred HTML tag for your
paragraph from the drop-down menu. An advantage of this is that paragraphs
assigned such tags take priority over other "body" tags (e.g., those using the <P>
tag) when appearing in search engine results (the H1 tag is the highest priority).

Using Site Manager

WebPlus's **Site Manager** hosts a whole range of useful site-wide information
available from a single menu-driven dialog. The tool lets you view Page/Master
Page Properties, and pick from a selection of Management tools for viewing and
editing hyperlinks (see below), resources, text, fonts, and much more.

Hyperlink		Se
Page:	📋 All Pages	
Type:	⅜ All Links ▼	

☐ Page ▲	Hyperlink	Linked To
☐ 🔲 Master A	Text "Nullam lorem sapien"	Page: Terms & Conditions
☐ 🔲 Master A	Text "Felis turpis hendrerit "	Page: Terms & Conditions
☐ 🏠 Home	Text "Read more "	Page: Products
☐ 🏠 Home	Text "Read more "	Page: About Us
☐ 🏠 Home	Text "Read more "	Page: Gallery
☐ 🏠 Home	Text "Read more "	Page: Gallery
☐ 🏠 Home	Text "Read more "	Page: Gallery
☐ 🏠 Home	Text "Read more "	Page: Links
☐ 🏠 Home	Text "Read more "	Page: Article 1
☐ 🔳 Contact	Text "name@company.com "	Mail: name@company.com

Powerful features of Site Manager include:

- The ability to control the scope and to manage an individual, a selection or all pages in your site equally.

- Any column can be sorted up or down which offers a quick way of reordering information.

- Find and Replace. Where available, this is a powerful way of applying text changes across all web pages simultaneously.

While most management tools are beneficial at any point in site development, the management of resources and text, as well as use of the Site Checker, are essential for checking your site just prior to web publishing.

To launch Site Manager:

- Click ⬚ **Site Manager** on the Hintline at the bottom of your workspace (or on the Pages context toolbar).

A quick summary gives an indication of what each management feature can do for you.

Type of Management	Lets you...
Page/Master Page Properties	Include pages in navigation, attach master pages, set page alignment and size, rename pages, set a background, add sounds, optimize pages for search engines, and apply redirections, transitions, or access control.
HTML Page Properties	View and edit HTML page names, file names (and path), include pages in navigation (with separator control), open in frame.
Hyperlink	View and edit hyperlinks, jump to hyperlinks on the page, find and replace destination links.
Anchor	View and edit anchor name and location, include pages in navigation (with separator control), jump to anchors.

Resource	View images, media, linked files, HTML code resources, scripts, or applets in your site. Jump to each resource on the page, swap between linked/embedded image status, replace or resample images.
E-Commerce	View E-Commerce objects on pages across your site.
Text	View and edit text (in WritePlus), name stories, reformat text, apply styles, convert creative frames and tables to HTML-compatible text.
Font	View fonts and their availability, jump to fonts on the page, and substitute fonts.
File	Display the site structure with page file names rather than page names. Add files to your site. Rename and move file locations.
Site checker	Display common layout problems discovered in your site.

Understanding pages and master pages

Looking at individual pages from a design standpoint, each WebPlus page has a "foreground" **page** and a "background" **master page**.

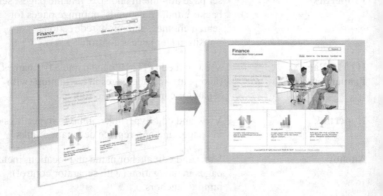

Master pages provide a flexible way to store background elements that you would like to appear on more than one page—for example a logo, background, header/footer, border design, or navigation bar. The key concept here is that a particular master page is typically shared by multiple pages, as illustrated below. By placing a design element on a master page and then assigning several pages to use that master page, you ensure that all the pages incorporate that element. Of course, each individual page can have its own elements.

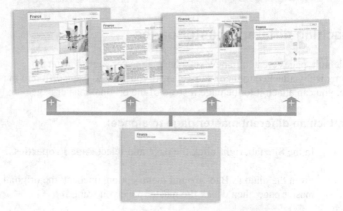

The Studio's **Site tab** includes an upper Master Pages section containing your master page(s), and a lower Site Structure in the Pages window containing your standard pages. Each page shown in the window indicates the master page being used for that page.

For more varied page designs across you site, you can create more than one master page (see Adding, removing, and rearranging pages on p. 50). Once you have multiple master pages, they can be attached to separate pages or in combination on the same page.

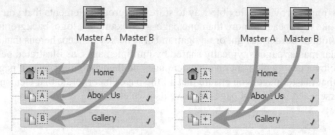

Attaching different master pages

By default, pages created in new sites have a master page (Master A) automatically attached to them. However, if you want to use a different master page, you can attach it to the page instead of the original master page.

To attach an different master page to a page:

1. In the Site tab, right-click the page and select **Page Properties...**.

   From the dialog's Background menu option, uncheck the original master page, then check the master page you want to use.

2. Click **OK**.

To detach a master page:

- Uncheck its entry in the Page Properties dialog (Background menu option).

Attaching multiple master pages

WebPlus lets you apply multiple master pages to the currently selected web page for more complex page-specific designs. This also lets you arrange the order of master pages in relation to each other and the page content itself.

As an example, let's say you have two designs existing on two separate master pages—"Master **A**" and "Master **B**". From Page Properties, you can place "Master B", containing the IPSUM text, in front of the selected page, with Master A used as the page background.

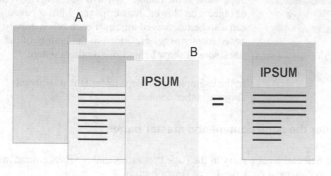

To attach multiple master pages to a web page:

1. In the Site tab, right-click the page and select **Page Properties...**.

2. From the dialog's Background menu option, check multiple master pages.

3. Click **OK**. The page will now be using the page elements of all master pages.

The Site tab's Site Structure shows a web page with a plus sign if multiple master pages are attached (instead of A, B, C, etc.).

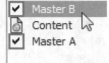

The above dialog also lets you control the order in which the page and master page contents are displayed on the page. In a similar way to layers in an illustration program, objects on the entry uppermost in the dialog's list will be shown in front of objects on "lower" master pages. Master pages can also be rearranged amongst each other. Newly added master pages are added to the bottom of the stack so will show behind of all other content.

In the example opposite, Master B is positioned above all other content.

To reorder the page content and master pages:

- Select the page entry in the Page Properties dialog (Background menu option) and click the **Up** or **Down** button.
  - or -

- Move a page by dragging its name to a new position in the list.
  - or -

- From the Objects tab, select a page, then reorder master pages by dragging.

Editing master page objects

If you're working on pages which have master pages attached, then **master page objects** will contribute to your page design. These objects can be edited quickly and easily from the page by using a control bar under the selected object.

To edit the master page object:

1. On your web page, select the master page object, to reveal the control bar

2. Click [icon] **Edit on Master Page**. The master page is displayed for editing.

On occasion, you may want to make a master page object on your page independent from its master page. These objects can become editable by being **promoted** from the master page to the web page, with the original master page object being replaced by a freely editable copy.

To promote a master page object:

1. On your web page, select the master page object, to reveal the control bar under the object.

2. Click [icon] **Promote from Master Page**. This makes a copy of the original object, which can then be edited independently without affecting the master page.

> [icon] All other pages using the master page will remain unaffected.

If you change your mind at any point you can reattach the object to the master page, leaving your page as it was originally.

To reattach object:

1. On your standard page, select the promoted object, to reveal the control bar under the object.

2. Click [icon] **Revert to Master Page**.

Adding, removing, and rearranging pages

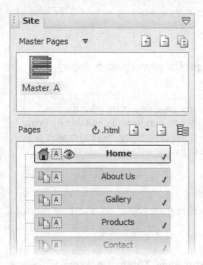

Using the Studio's Site tab, you can:

- Add standard or HTML pages.

- Delete pages.

- Add one or more master pages.

- Use drag-and-drop to rearrange pages within your site structure.

- Add pages from installed design templates.

- Add offsite links.

- Set a page to be the home page.

Use the upper Master Pages window of the Site tab to access master pages, and the Pages window (tab's central Site Structure tree) to access pages.

Besides the Site tab, WebPlus offers a variety of other ways to manipulate pages: the **Site Structure** dialog, the **Master Page Manager**, and both standard and right-click (context) menus.

Adding pages

To add a new blank page:

1. In the Pages Window (Site Structure tree) of the Studio's Site tab, select a page after which you want to add the new page.

2. Click the down arrow on the 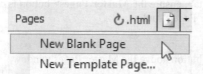 **Add** button directly above the Site tab's Pages window. From the drop-down menu, choose **New Blank Page**.

3. In the Page Properties dialog, specify options for the new page from each of the menu options in turn (see Setting page properties on p. 56).

4. Click **OK**.

A new page appears at the specified location in the site structure. The page uses Site Properties (p. 32) for its dimensions. You can always move the page to a different position or level, or switch to a different master page (see Rearranging pages or Attaching master pages on p. 53 and 46).

The Page Properties dialog allows pages to be placed anywhere in your site and have object copied from existing web pages via the Navigation and Appearance menu options, respectively.

Any new page created will use the currently set Site Properties (**File** menu), such as the default page size and alignment, unless you've overwritten site properties in the Page Properties dialog.

The "blank" page may also be based on a master page, e.g. if the site was created from a template, and may therefore contain page content as defined by the blank page's master page.

Adding master pages

To add a new master page:

1. On the Studio's Site tab, ensure the **Master Pages>** button is clicked to expand the Master Page Window.

2. Click the ⊞ **Add** button above the Master Pages window.

A new master page appears in the Site tab's Master Pages window.

💡 To reassign pages to particular master pages, see Understanding pages and master pages on p. 44.

Deleting pages

To delete a page or master page:

1. On the Studio's Site tab, select the page (or master page) to delete by clicking its entry.

2. Click the ⊟ **Remove** button above the appropriate window to delete the page.

🔖 When you delete a page, you'll have the option to **remove** any hyperlinks in your site that point to it, or **redirect** the hyperlinks to another specified page (hyperlinks to anchors on the deleted page can optionally be deleted).

Adding HTML pages

HTML pages can be added to any Site tab's Site Structure. Such pages can be included in navigation as for standard pages.

To add an HTML page:

1. In the Pages Window (Site Structure tree) of the Studio's Site tab, select a page after which you want to add the new page.

2. Click the down arrow on the ▾ **Add** button directly above the Pages window. From the drop-down menu choose **New HTML Page**.

A new HTML page is added to the Site tab. See Creating HTML pages (p. 59) for more information.

Rearranging pages

Besides using the Site Structure tree to add or delete pages, you can use it to rearrange pages as needed. Using the parent/child structure, rearranging pages is an intuitive process whether you use drag-and-drop or convenient buttons. You can move a page:

-   To a different sequential position (up or down) at the same level of the structure

-   To a higher (parent) level

-   To a lower (child) level

To move a page:

1. Display the Studio's Site tab.

2. Click to select the page in the Site Structure tree.

3. (Using drag-and-drop) Drag the page entry up or down and drop it at a new position in the tree. Watch the cursor for feedback on the new position relative to that of the page just below the cursor:

    moves the page to the same level as, and following, the highlighted target page.

    makes the page a child of the page below the highlighted target page.

Adding template pages

While adding standard pages lets you start page design from scratch, you can make life a little easier by adopting "ready to go" pages from your installed WebPlus templates. To maintain the page's original design, any master page associated with the added page is "imported" with the page.

To add a new page from a template:

1. In the Pages Window (Site Structure tree) of the Studio's Site tab, select a page after which you want to add the new page.

2. Click the down arrow on the ⬚ ▾ **Add** button directly above the Pages window. From the drop-down menu, choose **New Template Page...**.

3. From the **Add New Page from Template** dialog, select a template from the left-hand pane, and check the page for addition (check further pages for inclusion if needed).

4. WebPlus lets you control if an associated master page is copied with the page. Pick from the top-left drop-down menu choosing one of:

- **Copy Master Page**. To always copy the master page to your site.

- **Compare and Copy Master Page**. Checks if the master page already exists in your site then copies it if not present.

- **No Master Page**. The page's master page is never copied.

5. Click the **Open** button. The pages are added to the Site tab.

Adding offsite links

You can also add an **offsite link** to your site structure. Typically, this would be a page or resource separate from your site that you wanted to include in your site's navigation structure. The offsite link appears in the Site Structure tree and in navigation bars, so you can manipulate it just as if it were a page in your site.

To add an offsite link:

1. In the Pages Window (Site Structure tree) of the Studio's Site tab, select a page after which you want to add the new page.

2. Click the down arrow on the [ ] ▾ **Add** button above the Pages window. From the drop-down menu, choose **New Offsite Link...**.

3. In the dialog, type a **Menu name** to identify the offsite link in the Site Structure tree (the equivalent of its page name).

4. Click to select the link destination type, and enter the specific offsite hyperlink target (see Selecting a hyperlink target on p. 85), and the window in which you want the target to appear. Keep **Include in Navigation** checked if the link is to appear in site-wide navigation.

- Check **Before** and/or **After** to apply horizontal separator lines above/below the page as a submenu item in navigation bars.

- Add a **Description** to add extra page-related text on the bar's submenu item.

5. Click **OK**.

Setting your home page

To make a web page your home page:

- Right-click on a standard page in your Site tab then select **Set as Home Page**.

Setting page properties

Your WebPlus site has its own general framework, consisting of the **site** itself; one or more **master pages**; and a number of individual **pages**. Each aspect of the framework has various **property** settings that contribute to the look and behaviour or your site when it's published. Whether you start with a WebPlus template or from scratch, you can choose whether to stick with the default property settings or alter them to suit your needs.

Page properties of individual pages can be viewed either via the Site tab, by right-clicking on the active page in your workspace, or via the Site Manager. The Site Manager offers a more powerful method of not just viewing but modifying the properties of multiple pages at the same time—simply check your chosen pages and alter one or more page properties. All checked pages will adopt the new settings.

To view master page property settings:

- Click the   **Master Page Manager** button above the Master Pages window on the Site tab. The Master Page Manager appears.

To view normal web page property settings:

- Right-click the page in the workspace and choose **Page Properties...**.

The Page Properties dialog appears.

Tab name	Property
Navigation (default)	**Page, title, and file name** Each page has a "visible" page name or file name shown in Site tab's Site Structure tree. You can edit either, as well as choose a title different from the page name.

Include in navigation

By default, all pages are included in navigation bars. Use this option to exclude the page from navigation.

Separators and Description

If included in navigation, check **Before** and/or **After** to apply separator lines between both navigation bar menu options and pop-up menu options. A **Description** box adds extra page-related text information under the bar's submenu item.

Active document frame

Pages can be opened in an active document frame if the frame has been created previously.

Placement

This option places your new page before, after, or as a child of the page you choose in the drop-down list.

> This option only shows when you're adding a page.

Appearance   **Width and Height**

Sets the page dimensions for individual pages/master pages, overriding the **Default page size** dimensions (in **File>Site Properties...**) used when the page was created.

> You can also drag the right-hand or bottom page edge to change page width or height, respectively.

Page alignment

Alignment determines how the page content appears in a browser. Use the Site's default page alignment setting (Use Site setting), or choose Left or Centred as an override.

Selection

Choose a **Colour** which will uniquely distinguish objects placed on this page from those on an attached master page. The colour shows on object hover over and on the selected object's outline.

Copying

Duplicates the design elements from an existing web page onto your new page. Check **Copy objects from page** and select the page in the activated list. Attached HTML content can optionally be copied.

> This option only shows when you're adding a page.

Background   **Master pages**
Controls which master pages are attached to your page. Check to attach a master page, uncheck to detach, or drag (or use Up/Down buttons) to rearrange the master page order.

Background
The drop-down list offers different ways of displaying the page background.

- **Use site appearance**: Uses the site-wide background appearance as set in **File>Site Properties>Page**.

- **Use master page background**: Uses an attached master page's background settings. These settings will have overridden the site's background appearance (above).

- **Use custom background**: Uses an **On-page colour**, **Background colour**, or **Background Image** just for the current page. If Use custom background is selected, the options become available.

Search   **Search tags**
Include optional tag descriptions and keywords on individual pages, which override the site's search engine settings.

Search   **Sitemaps and robots**
Engine   Informs search engines or robots if they can crawl, analyze and index the current page. A Sitemap file will include the current page in indexing whereas a Robots meta tag (or a robots.txt file) will exclude the page. These settings override the site's search engine settings.

Page Security   **Page Security**
Apply access control to your web page(s) by assigning the page to a user group (see Access Control on p. 176).

Redirect   **Redirect to**
After a configurable time interval a web page is redirected to a new hyperlink destination (another page, image, email, etc.).

Effects   **Page Entry/Exit Transitions**
Page entry and exit transitions can be applied as you navigate from one web page to another.

Use Sound file
Choose a **background** sound to load and play automatically when a specific page is first displayed.

Creating HTML pages

HTML code is the underlying tagged code which your website visitor's Internet browser reads, interprets and formats your page according to the tags used. The code and tags used are the instructions to which a page will be formatted, and as such it is vital that the code is correctly structured and conforms to HTML convention.

WebPlus supports the development of web pages in HTML. You can add pages within the Site tab's Site Structure window—a distinct HTML page icon is shown.

HTML pages in the Site tab can be controlled in a similar way to standard pages, i.e. you can drag/drop, rename, preview, insert offline links to, estimate download time, or include the page in navigation. However, HTML pages do not have master pages associated with them. In addition, a double-click of the HTML page icon will launch the HTML page's Source window for HTML editing (rather than the WYSIWYG display of a standard page). In the Source window you'll see some basic HTML tags which, if you're an experienced HTML developer, will be very familiar to you!

```
<!DOCTYPE HTML PUBLIC "-//W3C//DTD HTML 4.01
<html>
<head>
<meta http-equiv="Content-Type" content="text
<meta name="Generator" content="Serif WebPlu
<title>%thistitle%</title>
</head>
<style type="text/css">
<!--
a:link {color: %hyperlink%;}
a:visited {color: %followed%;}
a:hover {color: %rollover%;}
a:active {color: %active%;}
-->
</style>
<body style="background: %background%;">
<p><a href="%home%">%homename%</a>
</body>
</html>
```

> There is no WYSIWYG view when you work with HTML source code directly.

From this point, editing of the "template" HTML structure is required. Typically, text is inserted (by typing or pasting) between the opening <body...> and closing </body> tags although the <head> section can also be edited; each paragraph in the <body> section starts and ends with the <p> and </p> tags, respectively. You can also insert annotation tokens into your HTML code (see Attaching HTML code on p. 123) via right-click (pick **Insert Token**). The remainder of the HTML code outside of the opening/closing body tags does not need to be altered.

> ⚠ Editing HTML code requires prior understanding of HTML language and its convention. Poor editing may result in corruption of your code on the page or site level.

If you're new to HTML and need to start with the basics, it's best to search for "HTML tutorials" in your favourite Internet search engine before tackling HTML editing in earnest.

To create an HTML page:

1. In the Pages Window (Site Structure tree) of the Studio's Site tab, select a page after which you want to add the new page. A click on the page's entry suffices to select the page (its page name will become bold); double-clicking also displays the page in the workspace.

2. Click the down arrow on the [↓] ▾ **Add new page or link** button directly above the Pages window. From the drop-down menu, choose **New HTML Page** to add a page after the original page.

To edit an HTML page's source:

- Double-click the HTML page (see above) in the Site tab's Site Structure and edit the displayed code.

If you want to discard all changes to the HTML code, select ⟲ **Clear Changes** on the context toolbar above the HTML window.

To Quick Publish the HTML page (for live checking):

- Click 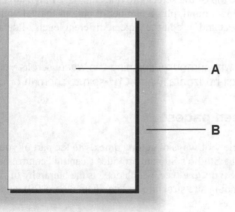 **Quick Publish to Web** on the context toolbar to publish the current page via your default FTP account.

To return to Design View:

- Select ✕ **Design View** on the context toolbar.

Viewing pages

The WebPlus workspace consists of a "page" area and a surrounding "pasteboard" area.

The **page** area (A) is where you put the text, graphics, and other elements that you want to appear on your final web page. The **pasteboard** (B) is where you generally keep elements that are being prepared or waiting to be positioned on the page area. When you publish your site from the WebPlus site, anything which overlaps the page area appears, while anything entirely on the pasteboard does not. The pasteboard is shared by all pages and master pages, and it's useful for copying or moving objects between pages.

To move or copy an object between pages via the pasteboard:

1. Drag the object from the source page onto the pasteboard (hold down the **Ctrl** key to copy).

2. Display the target page (see Switching between pages below).

3. Drag (or **Ctrl**-drag to copy) the object from the pasteboard onto the target page.

WebPlus makes it easy to see exactly what you're working on—from a wide view of a whole page to a close up view of a small region. For example, you can use the **scroll bars** at the right and bottom of the main window to move the page and pasteboard with respect to the main window. The view automatically re-centres itself as you drag objects to the edge of the screen.

The **View toolbar** at the top of the screen provides the ![hand] **Pan Tool** as an alternative way of moving around, plus a number of buttons that let you zoom in and out so you can inspect and/or edit the page at different levels of detail.

> ☿ If you're using a wheel mouse, spinning the wheel scrolls vertically. **Shift**-spin to scroll horizontally and **Ctrl**-spin to zoom in or out!

Switching between pages

WebPlus provides a variety of ways of getting quickly to the part of your site you need to work on. The Studio's Site tab provides a central "control panel" including both the **Site Structure tree**, which depicts the hierarchy of pages in your site (see Understanding site structure and navigation on p. 29), and icons for the site's **master pages**.

Selecting vs. viewing a page: Single-clicking a page/master page entry merely **selects** the page. To actually **view** the associated page/master page you need to **double-click** an entry.

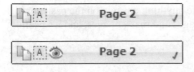

An orange entry (with bolded page name) denotes the **selected** page.

The eye icon denotes the **currently viewed** page—which you're able to edit in the workspace. This example shows that the pa is currently in view as well as selected.

Master A

A highlighted master page icon in the Site tab's upper window denotes the **selected** master page.

Master A

An eye icon in the master page icon denotes the currently viewed page. This example shows a viewed as well as selected master page.

To view a specific page/master page:

Several methods can be used to view a page:

- On the Hintline, use the Hintline's ◀ ▶ page navigation buttons.
  - or -
  Click the entry for the page or master page in the **Page Locator** list.

- On the Studio's **Site** tab, double-click the entry for the page (or master page) you want to view. The Site Structure window of the tab includes a tree with entries for pages in the site, while the Master Pages window shows only master pages as thumbnails. You may need to click the **Master Pages>** button to display the master pages window.

- Click the ▤ **Site Structure** button on the Hintline or on the Site tab's Page window. Select the page entry in the dialog's tree (double-click tree entries if necessary to expand each branch). Then click the **View Page** button.

For master pages:

- On the Studio's **Site** tab, click the **Master Pages>** button to reveal a master page window. One or more master page icons will be displayed.

- Double-click the icon for the master page you want to view.

To switch between the current page and master page:

- Click the **Page/Master Page** button on the Hintline.

> ✎ If multiple master pages are attached to a page, only the first master page is switched to.

As a shortcut to view the site's Home page:

- Click the **Home Page** button on the Hintline.

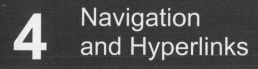

4 Navigation
and Hyperlinks

Adding navigation bars

In WebPlus, **navigation bars** are programmed to understand your site structure, making it easy to design a site that's simple to navigate.

Navigation bars facilitate movement between the various sections and levels of a site (see p. 29), providing links to your Home page and other top-level section pages, while pop-up menus link to child pages within each section.

In the varied navigation bar examples above, the pages in your site make up the navigation bar options, with any "second-level" child pages, such as Product 1 and Product 2, showing as pop-up menus (shown on the front-most navigation bar only).

You can easily install navigation bars at any level of your site, reconfigure them to link to a particular part of the site, change the appearance of the navigation bar, and exclude particular pages from navigation as needed.

Levels and site structure

You may like to review Understanding site structure and navigation (p. 29) to remind yourself of how site structure is based on section and levels.

When you define a navigation bar, you can choose the page level that is displayed in your navigation bar. Think of this as a pointer to parts of the site that should be linked to, relative to the navigation bar's page. You can specify "Top Level", "Same Level", "Child Level", "Previous/Next", and more.

To help you understand this relationship between pages and these referenced levels, a visual clue is provided as you create your navigation bar (in each Navigation Type thumbnail). The dark rectangles show the page level to be used and the black dot (•), the page on which your navigation bar is placed.

| *Top* | *Same* | *Child* | *Previous* |
| *Level* | *Level* | *Level* | *and Next* |

> The icon designs are examples and do not represent the actually structure of your site.

Because navigation bars "understand" your site structure, they update dynamically if pages are moved to different levels!

Creating navigation bars

Navigation bars can be added to any page but are typically added to the master page—as this saves you the trouble of pasting the same element to multiple pages. A navigation bar on a master page behaves *as if it's on each page*—consistent with the notion that its buttons and menus are relative to where each page sits in the overall site structure.

When adding a navigation bar, you can choose how your navigation will appear on your page by choosing:

- **Type**: The intrinsic design of your navigation bar (e.g., block, speech, traditional).

- **Navigation Type**: The site or custom structure on which the navigation bar is based.

- **Appearance**: The button, separator, and background design of the navigation bar. Either preset or custom designs can be used.

- **Pop-Up menus**: The button, separator, and background design for any pop-up menus displaying off the navigation bar (if using child pages in your site structure).

To add a navigation bar:

1. Select the page (or master page).

2. From the **Web Objects** toolbar's ⊞▾ Navigation flyout, click ⊞
   Insert Navigation Bar.

3. From the dialog's **Type** tab, browse navigation bar types in the **Type**
   drop-down list, expanding menu options if needed. Use the keyboard
   arrows for quick browsing!

   In the adjacent preview window, hover over menu options to review
   the appearance of pop-up menus.

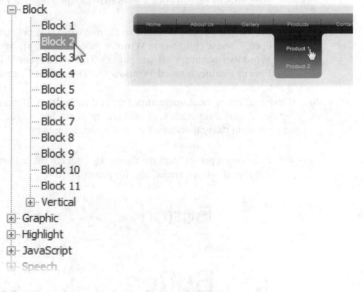

4. Select your chosen navigation type, e.g. Block 2.

5. From the **Navigation Type** tab choose whether to base your
   navigation bar directly on the site's Site Structure (enable **Based on
   site structure**).

   - or -

   Customize the navigation bar's options (enable **Custom**; see
   Customizing navigation bars on p. 71).

If choosing Site Structure, you can:

- Select which buttons should be included in the navigation bar: **Top Level**, **Parent Level**, **Same Level**, etc.

- Depending on the main selection, you can opt to include the **child page**, **anchors**, **home page**, **parent page,** and/or **Hide current page** or **disable links**.

- Enable a **Naming relative links** option if using relative links such as Home, Up, Previous and Next. With **Use fixed names** enabled, the relative names are shown, e.g., "Next"; **Use page names** displays the actual page name as defined in the page's properties. You can click **Customize** to edit a relative link name.

- Set **Target Frame/Window** to change where the new page will open. Choose from **Same Window** (most common), **New Window** (useful for off-site pages), **Top of Current Window**, **Parent Frame**, **Named Window** and **Document Frame**.

6. (Optional) From the **Appearance** tab, you can select different designs for your buttons, separators, or background if needed. These will show on your main navigation bar. You can select designs by:

- Choosing a preset from the flyout, by clicking the button thumbnail's down arrow, e.g. for preset buttons.

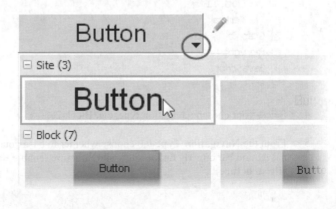

- or -

- Clicking *✎* **Edit** to create your own custom design, based on the currently selected button. You'll be able to change text font, size, and colour, along with backgrounds in several button states See WebPlus Help for more information.

7. (Optional) From the **Pop-Up Menus** tab, choose designs as described for Appearance tab, but which relate to "child" pages in your site structure.

8. Click **OK**. The navigation bar appears on your page.

💡 Navigation bar are colour schemed, allowing further control of the bar's appearance. See Using colour schemes on p. 321.

To edit a navigation bar:

1. Double-click the navigation bar.
   - or -

   Select 🔲 **Edit Navigation Bar...**.
   - or -

   Right-click the bar and choose **Edit Navigation Bar...**.

2. Change settings available from each tab.

Customizing navigation bar structure

By default, the navigation bar's structure will be based on your site structure. If you're looking to rearrange the order or hierarchy of your navigation bar items to be different from your Site Structure, WebPlus will allow you to customize any navigation bars by creating a **custom navigation tree**. You can add, edit, or delete elements which will access a range of link destination types (see Adding hyperlinks and anchors on p. 85) just as in Site tab's Site Structure.

🖉 Once you're working with a custom navigation tree, the navigation bar will no longer automatically update when new pages are added to your site. If you still want this to happen, you'll have to base your bar on the site's Site Structure.

To customize a selected navigation bar:

1. Double-click the navigation bar.

2. From the Navigation Type tab, enable the **Custom** option.

3. Rearrange the order of the navigation bar items by drag and drop (or use the **Move Up**, **Move Down**, **Make Child** or **Make Parent** buttons).

4. Click **Add Link** to add a new link to the end of your custom navigation tree, typically to add a page you've subsequently added to your site. The element is assigned a link destination, a target frame or window and a title in the displayed dialog. Click **OK**.

5. Click **OK** again. The navigation bar now uses the custom navigation tree to present menu options.

Click **Reset** to revert the navigation tree back to the site's structure or **Delete All** to remove all entries in the custom tree.

The custom navigation tree can also be saved in your site, for use in other navigation bars.

To save your customized navigation bar:

- Click **Defaults**, then choose **Save...** from the flyout.

- Enter a name for your custom Navigation tree (e.g., customnavtree-1).

- Click **OK**. The tree is stored in your site.

At a later date, for other navigation bars you can retrieve your saved tree, via **Defaults** (Load flyout).

Changing buttons, separators, and backgrounds

When you create or edit a navigation bar, you may wish to keep the bar's navigation type and structure the same, but change or customize buttons, separators, and the background that makes up the navigation bar.

New bars can be created from any existing navigation bar in your site. Simply choose a navigation bar first. This may help you achieve the desired appearance more quickly.

To display button, separator, and background settings:

- From the **Appearance** tab, you can change or customize buttons, separators, and the background by selecting the navigation bar element from a selection box.

> Buttons
> Separators
> Background

The dialog options subsequently change according to what navigation bar element is selected.

To change navigation bar buttons (for another preset button):

1. Click the drop-down arrow on the **Single** thumbnail to reveal a Presets flyout.

2. Select a button from a category (these match the navigation bar **Type** categories).

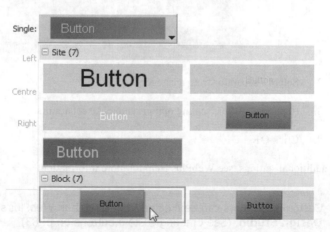

3. (Optional) Adjust **Separation** and **Alignment** options. Horizontal options affect buttons presented horizontally in the navigation bar, and vice versa.

4. Click **OK**.

See WebPlus Help for more information.

> Custom buttons can be created from scratch in WebPlus's **Button Studio**. (See Creating custom buttons on p. 83).

To change navigation bar separators (for another preset):

1. Click the drop-down arrow on the **Separator** thumbnail to reveal a Presets flyout.

2. Select a separator from a category.

3. (Optional) Adjust scaling options and make separators.

4. Click **OK**.

For additional settings, see WebPlus Help for more information.

> Custom separators can be created from scratch in WebPlus's **Design Studio**. (See Creating custom buttons on p. 83).

To change navigation bar background (for another preset):

1. Click the drop-down arrow on the **Background** thumbnail to reveal a Presets flyout.

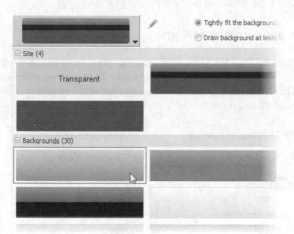

2. Select a background from a category.

3. (Optional) Adjust padding and other options to suit you design.

4. Click **OK**.

See WebPlus Help for more information.

Changing pop-up menus

Pop-up menus are an integral part of navigation bars that are based on site structures using child pages. They only appear when hovering over navigation bar buttons, and disappear when moving away from the button.

Like buttons, pop-up menus are highly configurable. One difference is that they can be configured as either **Text pop-up menus** and **Graphical pop-up menus**. The Navigation bar Type (Block, Highlight, Speech, etc.) can use either type of pop-up menu depending on the design.

To display pop-up menu settings:

1. From the **Pop-Up Menus** tab, you can customize your pop-up menu by choosing a menu type. Enable either **Text pop-up menus** or **Graphical pop-up menus**. The latter implements buttons objects to make up its menus.

   ⊙ Text pop-up menus   ○ Text pop-up menus

   ○ Graphical pop-up menus   ⊙ Graphical pop-up menus

   | Menu Text |
   | Margin |
   | Lines and Border |
   | Effects |
   | Size and Position |

   | Buttons |
   | Separators |
   | Background |
   | Effects |
   | Size and Position |

2. Select a menu option. The dialog options subsequently change according to the option selected.

3. Edit input boxes, drop-down lists, radio buttons, and check boxes to suit your pop-up menu design. Graphical pop-up menu settings for buttons, separators, and background share similar settings to those of buttons.

For settings in detail, see WebPlus Help or Graphical pop-up menu settings for more information.

Displaying separators

For any pages, offsite link, or anchor included in navigation and appearing on your navigation bar (or in its pop-up menus), you can control the display of separators between each menu option. See WebPlus Help.

Saving navigation bar options

If you've customized a navigation bar's buttons, separators, background, and its pop-up menu you can save these combined settings to a single location using the **Defaults** button. This is useful for applying the same navigation bar appearance to other navigation bars you create in your site.

Including/excluding pages in navigation

By default, all pages are **included in navigation**—that is, they can be linked to by navigation bars. You can **exclude** certain pages (any but the Home page) so they'll be ignored by navigation bars. For example, suppose you had a section of reference or archival pages that you didn't want visitors to explore top-down. Excluding the parent page for that section would remove it from the navigation bar. Note that excluding the page from navigation doesn't remove it from the site—the page will still appear in the Site Structure tree and you can still install hyperlinks to it; it just won't show up in a navigation bar.

To exclude a page from navigation:

- On the Studio's **Site** tab, right-click the page in the Site Structure tree and choose **Page Properties...**. Uncheck **Include in Navigation.**

- Included pages show a ✓ mark in their page entry in the Site tab's Site Structure tree, while excluded page entries lack the mark and appear greyed out.

Using dynamic navigation bars

Up to now, we've assumed that navigation bars are based on your site structure and show static pages as menu items. However, for more dynamic navigation bars, you can populate your navigation bar submenus with ever-changing forum, CMS, and blog article titles—simply click a title to view the relevant article.

We'll assume you're already using an offsite link to connect to your forum, CMS, and blog, and that the offsite link is included in navigation.

To create a dynamic navigation bar:

- Right-click the offsite link in Site tab and click **Offsite Link Properties...**.

- From the Offsite Link dialog, change the drop-down menu in the Smart Object Information section to add feed items (i.e., published article titles) as children to the bar's submenu.

Just add a link ▼
Just add a link
Add feed items as children of link
Replace link with feed items

Each article title is clickable, launching the associated article in a window, typically a separate window.

Converting to Panels

You can convert your navigation bar to a panel (p. 78), taking advantage of more freeform positioning of your navigation bar buttons (within the panel area) and the option to keep navigation bars visible at all times.

To convert a navigation bar to a panel:

1. Select the navigation bar.

2. From the context toolbar, select **Convert to Panel**.

For more information about panels, see Inserting panels on p. 106.

Adding pop-up menus

Pop-up menus form an integral part of multi-level navigation bars (p. 67), showing as menus that display only on button hover over. The pop-up menu items represent child pages at lower levels of your site.

In WebPlus, you can also add pop-up menus to any object (a QuickShape, image, a gallery item, but most typically a button), the menu being essentially the same as those integrated with navigation bars. Like navigation bars, the pop-up menu items that display can be configured, either adopting the entire site structure (or part of it) or your own custom structure.

Pop-up menus are especially useful when you may want to show a limited, perhaps related, set of navigation links such as a set of products.

You have full control of what level of your site your want to present in the pop-up menu. In the example opposite, the pop up menu is based on child pages belonging to a Products parent page (which would probably host the button and pop-up menu).

To create a pop-up menu:

1. Select an object to attach the pop-up menu to.

2. Select **Pop-Up Menu...** from the **Insert** menu.
   - or -

   Right-click an object and select **Pop-Up Menu...**.

3. From the dialog's **Navigation Type** tab, check the **Show a pop-up menu...** option to enable navigation links to be associated with the object.

4. Enable **Based on site structure** or **Custom** to either use your site's navigation links as part of the menu (below) or base the pop-up menu on your own custom structure (p. 71), respectively.

☑ Show a pop-up menu of navigation links for this object

⦿ Based on site structure   ○ Custom

Top Level   Parent Level

Home   Up

Same Level As...   Child Pages Of...

📄 Products   ▼

5. From the dialog's **Menu Appearance** tab, select **Text pop-up menus** or **Graphical pop-up menus**. The latter implements buttons objects to make up its menus.

6. Select a menu option from the box, then edit input boxes, drop-down lists, radio buttons, and check boxes to suit your pop-up menu design. Graphical pop-up menu settings for buttons, separators, and background share similar settings to those of buttons.

   All options are described in detail in Changing pop-up menus on p. 75.

7. Click **OK**.

Adding buttons

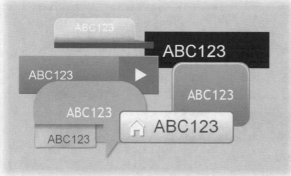

Buttons are an integral part of WebPlus navigation bars (see p. 67) but can also be added as independent objects onto your web page, either linking to a hyperlink destination or displaying a pop-up menu.

In WebPlus, buttons can be based on either a preset design or can be created from scratch in the Button Studio. It's quite common to choose a preset and then customize it to fit your requirements.

Whichever you choose, you'll be able to edit the text label to suit your button function simply and easily.

To add a preset button:

1. From the **Web Objects** toolbar's [icon] Navigation flyout, click [icon] **Insert Button**.

2. From the **Edit Button** dialog, click the button preview box.

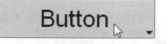

3. Select a preset button type from the flyout.

The preview box updates with your chosen button design.

4. Enter a **Button Label** to identify the button, such as "Home", "Images", "Help", etc.

5. Select an **Action** which will be invoked when the button is clicked.

- **Hyperlink** will direct the user to a target (e.g., Internet page, site page, file) via a hyperlink (see p. 85). Click **Edit...** to choose the target type and its destination and target window.

- **Submit Form** creates a Submit button used for submitting form data. The button label will always be overwritten to be Submit (but you can still edit it again). The Action for the button is actually invoked when the button is placed on a form.

- **Reset Form** creates a Reset button used on forms to clear data input in form fields. Submit and Reset buttons are usually placed side by side.

- **Custom Script** lets you type your own JavaScript code into the input box (you don't need to include the <script language="JavaScript"> and </script> tags).

6. (Optional) Check **Disabled** to make the control inactive unless activated by script.

7. (Optional) Check **Button initially in Down state** to make the button appear as if it has been already clicked (as opposed to being in Normal state).

8. Click **OK**.

9. Position the cursor at the chosen cursor position where you want to place your button.

10. To insert the button at a default size, simply click the mouse to.
    - or -
    To set the size of the button, drag out a region and release the mouse button.

To edit a button:

*   Double-click a button and edit as described above.

Creating custom buttons

If you're looking to further modify your chosen button preset (or work from scratch) you can use **Button Studio**, a button design environment integrated into WebPlus. This allows you to focus on your button design without the distractions of other objects on the page, i.e. the design is displayed in isolation.

The Button Studio lets you edit your custom button's appearance in each of its button states, i.e. initially in its **Normal** state, when pressed **Down**, and during **Hover** over.

⚲ Button Studio is equipped with an interactive **How To tab** to assist you as you create your custom button. The tab includes further information about editing in different button states and using guides and stretching options to control which button elements are stretched or kept as is.

To create a custom button:

1. (Optional) From the Button dialog, select a button preset from which to base your new button.

2. From the same dialog, click the ✎ **Edit** button. Button Studio is launched with your button zoomed in to fit your workspace.

3. In Normal state (see Button States tab), use standard WebPlus tools and tabs to customize your button design to your liking.

4. From the Button States tab at the bottom of your workspace, repeat for each state (select Down, Hover, Disabled, etc.) to edit your button in each state.

    The Menu Right and Menu Below options are for Pop-Up menus only.

5. Click **Commit Changes** on the main toolbar to exit. The modified button is updated in its original position.

⚲ How do I edit my text? The Button Studio focuses on button design rather than the labelling. To edit the label, double click the button on the page and edit again in the dialog's **Button Label** option.

Once you've added your button to the page you can still use Button Studio to modify its design at any time.

To edit a button design:

*   Select ⬉ **Edit Button Design** from the context toolbar.

Converting to Navigation Bar

You can convert your button to a navigation bar (p. 67) at any time, making it possess the characteristics inherent in all navigation bars, i.e. it will present your site structure (or a custom structure).

To convert a button to a navigation bar:

1. Select the button.

2. From the context toolbar, select **Convert to Navigation Bar**.

Adding hyperlinks and anchors

Hyperlinking an object such as a box, some text, or a picture means that a visitor to your website can click on the object to trigger an event. The event is most commonly a jump to one of the following:

- Site page

- Internet page (somewhere on the web)

- Email composition window

- File on your local disk or network

- Anchor (a designated target within a web page)

- Smart object (forum, blog or CMS)

- RSS feed or podcast

- Shopping cart

- Navigation element

- User Data

- Picture

Well-designed hyperlinks are an important aspect of site structure. They help visitors navigate through your site and serve as an important adjunct to logical page relationships as shown in the Site Structure tree. (But don't overlook the time-saving advantages of using navigation bars.)

> You can manage all hyperlinks and anchors throughout your site by using the **Site Manager**, accessible from the Default context toolbar or Hintline.

To add a hyperlink: :

1. Use the **Pointer Tool** to select the single or grouped object or highlight the region of text to be hyperlinked.

2. Select **Hyperlink** from the **Tools** toolbar's Hyperlink flyout.

   The Hyperlinks dialog appears.

3. Click to select the link destination type, i.e. a Site Page, Internet Page, Smart Object, etc.

4. Depending on the link type, choose type-specific options in the right-hand pane as your **hyperlink target**.

5. A range of target windows or frames can be chosen depending on how you want the link destination to be displayed. The types (along with expected results) are:

   - **Same Window**: the link destination is shown in the same window from which the hyperlink was clicked.

   - **New Window**: A new window is used to display the link destination.

   - **Top of Current Window**: the link destination is shown in the top level window. Use for hyperlinks created within frames.

   - **Parent Frame**: the link destination is shown in the Parent Frame or Parent Window of the frame from which the hyperlink was clicked. Use for hyperlinks created within a frame on a page (or for frames within frames). (See online Help.)

- **Named Window**: A custom window can be defined by entering a new window name in the right-most drop-down menu.

- **Document Frame**: The link destination is shown in a previously created frame (using the Framed Document Tool). The HTML ID (e.g., ifrm_1) of any existing frame is selected from the right-most drop-down menu. (See online Help).

  If you're targeting an active document frame, select the active frame from the **Open in active document frame** drop-down list. If it doesn't show in the list you'll need to set the frame to be "active" by double-clicking the frame and checking **Active Document Frame**.

- **Lightbox**: The link destination is shown in a pop-up lightbox superimposed over your web page. Click **Lightbox Options...** to optionally provide a caption, change lightbox dimensions, or include as part of a slideshow. See Using lightboxes on p. 103.

6. Choose other properties such as **Title** name (shown as hover-over text describing the hyperlink destination) and a shortcut access key.

7. Use the **Style** drop-down list to choose how text hyperlink is formatted (if text is being hyperlinked).

8. Click **OK**.

To modify or remove a hyperlink:

1. Use the **Pointer Tool** to select the object, or click for an insertion point inside the linked text. (It's not necessary to drag over a hyperlinked region of text.)

2. Click the 🔗 **Hyperlink** button on the **Tools** toolbar's Hyperlink flyout.

The Hyperlinks dialog appears with the current link target shown. If the link is in text, the whole text link highlights.

- To modify the hyperlink, select a new link destination type, target, and/or options.

- To remove the hyperlink, click **No Hyperlink**.

To view or edit existing hyperlinks:

- Choose **Site Manager>Hyperlink Manager...** on the **Tools** menu to view, rename, or remove hyperlinks.

Inserting an anchor

An anchor is a specific location on a page that can serve as the target for a hyperlink. Invisible to the web page visitor, it typically marks a point within some text (such as the start of a particular section) or an image at some point down the page.

To insert an anchor:

1. Use the **Pointer Tool** to select the target object, or click for an insertion point inside the target text.

2. Click the ⚓ **Anchor** button on the **Tools** toolbar's Hyperlink flyout.
   - or -
   Choose **Anchor...** from the **Insert** or right-click menu.

3. In the dialog, type a name for the anchor.

4. (Optional) Check **Include Anchor in Navigation** to allow the anchor (typically a selected object) to be accessed via a navigation bar instead of a hyperlink. You'll need to check **Include anchors** on your navigation bar first. Give the anchor a title.

   - Check **Before** and/or **After** to apply horizontal separator lines above/below the anchor as a submenu item in navigation bars.

   - Add a **Description** to add extra page-related text information on the bar's submenu item.

5. Click **OK**.

To view or edit existing anchors:

- Choose **Site Manager>Anchor Manager...** on the **Tools** menu to view, rename, or remove an anchor attached to a particular object.

5 Adding
Web Objects

Adding a site search

WebPlus uses a powerful search facility which matches user search terms with text that appears in your site in artistic text, text frames or tables. This makes it easy to retrieve content from any hosted web pages.

The search feature works by using the **Site Search Tool** and **Site Search Results Tool**, both hosted on the **Web Objects** toolbar's Search flyout. Each tool is used to create objects that work together in combination.

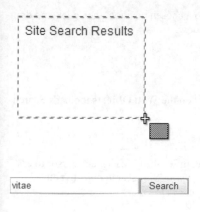

Site Search Results object—creates a window in which the search results are displayed. Typically, this is placed and sized onto its own page, and does not appear in the site navigation structure.

You'll normally position the search results box ahead of adding the Site Search object.

Site Search object—the text box in which users type the word or phrase they want to search for. This text box is usually added to a master page and appears on all pages of the site.

As an example, the above search term "vitae" could retrieve search results showing web pages which contain the search term. The user clicks the **Search** button to initiate any search.

Products
In eget sapien vitae Vivamus vel sapien.
Maecenas Curabitur Nulla vestibulum ele
nisl ...

Downloads
SoftwareDownloads Latest Reviews In e
Morbi pellentesque Mauris purus Donec M
Vivamus...

Services
Services List Overview Services List Aliq
neque. Donec posuere tempus massa. C
ornare non, v...

The search results show a hyperlinked page name heading plus associated web page text for reference. Simply click the hyperlink to access the web page.

To add Site Search Results:

1. Click the **Site Search Results Tool** on the **Web Objects** toolbar's Search flyout.

2. Move the ⊹ place cursor to a chosen position, then click and drag to place your search results window.

To add the Site Search object:

1. Click the **Site Search Tool** on the **Web Objects** toolbar's Search flyout.

2. On the web page or master page, move the ⊹ place cursor to a chosen position and click to place your Site Search object. Your search object appears on the page.

> Add the search object to the top of your master page to allow site-wide access to the search feature.

Site search is useless without some means of displaying the search results to the user. This is possible by using the Site Search Results object which, like the Site Search object, can be placed on a web page under a place cursor. However, the object is typically resized to full page size before placement (it needs to display multiple web page hits consecutively).

> Keep the search results on a separate, perhaps new, page which can also have its own look and feel (double-click the object to alter page appearance).

Using the Gallery

The **Gallery tab** is packed with professionally designed drag-and -drop creative content which will give your website that modern look! A whole range of categories are available, including:

- Picture Frames

- Badges & Stickers

- E-Commerce Buttons

- Flags

- Flash Banners

- Icon Sets and Icons

- Notes

- Quick Symbols

The tab also serves as a container for storing your own design objects you'd like to reuse in the same or different websites. Once you've copied a design to the Gallery, it becomes available to any site—simply open the Gallery!

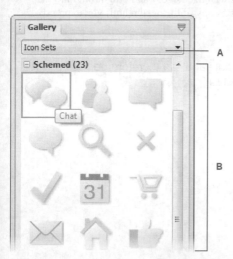

The Gallery has two parts: an upper **Categories** drop-down list (**A**) and a lower **Designs** window (**B**) showing a list of thumbnails representing the designs in the selected category.

To view your Gallery:

1. Click the Studio's **Gallery** tab.

2. Select a category from the drop-down menu.

My Designs
My Designs
Badges & Stickers
E-Commerce Buttons
Flags
Flash Banners
Icon Sets
Icons
Logos
Notes
Picture Frames
Quick Symbols
Quotes
Ribbons
Smilies

The items from the first listed sub category are displayed by default.

To use a design from the Gallery:

- Click its thumbnail in the design category and drag it out onto the page. The Gallery retains a copy of the design until you expressly delete it.

Some gallery items are editable and can therefore be used as the starting point for your own designs.

Storing your own designs

The Gallery tab can also store your own **custom** designs in the ready-to-go **My Designs** category—the design is made available in any WebPlus site.

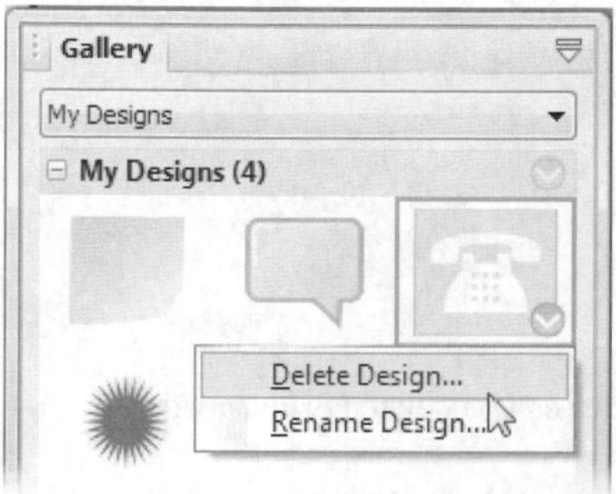

When you first install WebPlus, the My Designs gallery will be empty, ready for custom designs to be added to it.

To move or copy an object into the My Designs category:

1. Select the My Designs category from the **Categories** drop-down list.
2. Drag the object from the page and drop it onto the Designs window.
3. From the dialog, enter a name for your design, then select **OK**. A thumbnail of the design appears in the Designs window.

Press the **Ctrl** key before starting to drag to copy rather than move your design.

To rename or delete a design:

- Click on the drop-down button in the bottom-right corner of a thumbnail (shown by hover over) and choose from the menu.

To further categorize your designs, you can optionally add sub categories to My Designs (below) or create a new custom category instead of My Designs.

Once created, sub categories and categories can be deleted or renamed.

To add, delete, or rename custom sub categories:

- ⬇ To add, select a category and click **Add Sub Category...** from the tab's **Tab Menu** button.

- To delete or rename, select options from the ⊙ drop-down button on the sub category title bar.

If adding a sub category, you need to name it in a dialog. For renaming or deletion, simply pick the sub category in advance of picking the option.

To add, delete, or rename custom categories:

1. With the Gallery tab selected, click the ⬇ **Tab Menu** button and choose **Add category...**, **Remove category**, or **Rename category...** from the flyout menu.

2. Use the dialog to enter and/or confirm your change.

⚠ All designs in a deleted category will also be lost.

Adding Google Maps

Use embedded **Google Maps** in your web page if want to make sure that a client can locate your headquarters, attendees can find that special meeting (or event), or identify special interest locations. By embedding in a purposely designed "Directions" web page, you'll be able to add the map and written supporting directions to your site accordingly.

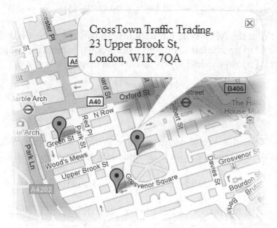

Each map will allow **markers** to be placed on the map to identify each location. Each marker can be made to pop up (on clicking) one of the following:

- a callout box offering plain text (e.g., a postal and/or web address).

- a callout box offering HTML-formatted text.

- a StreetView window.

To add a Google Map:

1. Click   **Insert Google Map** on the **Web Objects** toolbar's Media flyout.

2. From the Google Map dialog, enter your zip code, post code, or address in the **Search for a location** field, then click **Search**. As Google's geolocator is being used, WebPlus will sense your locale, and display local addresses preferentially.

3. Navigate around the map using supporting panning and zoom controls—drag the hand cursor to pan, the zoom slider and buttons to magnify/zoom out. If you've got a mouse with a scroll wheel, ensure **Enable mouse scroll wheel zoom** is checked for optimum zoom control.

4. (Optional) From the **Navigation control** drop-down list, select Full (for panning, Zoom buttons, and Zoom slider), Compact (for Zoom buttons only), or None (to hide all navigation controls).

5. (Optional) From the **Map type Control** drop-down list, select Bar (for side-by-side Map and Satellite options), drop-down Menu (for Map, Satellite, and Terrain modes), or None (to hide map type controls).

6. Click **OK**.

7. ⊹ ▨ You'll see the mouse pointer change to the **Paste** cursor. What you do next determines the initial size and placement of the map.

   To insert the map at the default size, simply click the mouse.
   - or -
   To set the size of the map to better fit your page design, drag out a region and release the mouse button.

🔖 The 👤 Street View icon can be dragged onto your map to display the location under you cursor in Street View. Click to ✕ exit the Street View window. If you don't want this feature available to web visitors, uncheck **Show Street Control** in the dialog.

Adding markers

 You can add an unlimited number of red markers to your Google Map. Each markers can display further details on hover over and mouse click.

To add a marker:

1. From the Google Map dialog, click **Add**.

2. Place the $-{}^{|}_{|}-$ cursor over the chosen location, then click.

3. From the Google Map Marker dialog, enter a **Name** for the marker. This "tooltip" displays on **hover over** and could represent a company or site name.

4. Assign a **Click action** to the marker, i.e. what gets displayed on button click. Select one of the following:

    -   Default Label: text is entered into the **Label** box. On publishing, a click displays plain text in a callout box.

    -   Treat label as script: text is entered with HTML tags into the Label box. On publishing, a click displays an HTML-formatted callout box.

    -   Street view: On publishing, a maximized Street View window is displayed in front of your map. Click to ⊠ exit the Street View window.

5. Click **OK**. The marker appears on the map preview in green (to indicate it is currently selection). Repeat the process for each marker in turn.

At some point, you may want to edit, locate, move, or delete a marker on your Google Map.

To edit your Google Map markers:

-   Double-click the Google Map on your page.

-   From the dialog, select a marker from the **Map Markers** drop-down list, then:

    -   To edit the marker label, click **Edit** and modify the text in the **Label** scrolling box.

- To move the marker, click **Move**, then place the $^{-}_{\,\,\,\,\,\,}$ cursor on the map again.

- To delete the marker, click **Remove**.

To record your Street view setting:

1. With **Click action** set to Street view, use window pan and zoom controls to set your view; this sets the direction (**Heading**), angle (**Pitch**), and magnification (**Zoom**).

2. Click **Record view**.

Adding advertising

Google Adsense is a free Google service which allows you to place advertising space on your web pages. Visitors to your pages will be served adverts according to the type of content your site is publishing—the visitor benefits from easy access to tailored shopping opportunities while you, as web developer, earn money to offset the cost of hosting or to get rich quick!

To advertise, web developers must have an approved Google Adsense account (www.google.com/adsense), where you'll be able to choose the type and format of advert to be displayed, each advert being called a **unit**. You can copy and paste a generated code snippet **per unit** from the Google Adsense website and paste it into WebPlus's Google Adsense advertisement dialog.

The types of advert include basic Ad, Image, Link, and Video Units. Formats differ according to unit type but these range from Leaderboard (728x90 pixel), Banner (468x60), Half Banner (234x60), Button (125x125), to various Skyscraper, square, and rectangular sizes.

Google Adsense also offers comprehensive usage reports, account management, a filtering, and supporting resources. For more information, visit www.google.com/adsense.

To log in to Google Adsense:

- Visit **www.google.com/adsense** to sign up or sign in to Google Adsense. Click the **Sign Up Now** button if you're a new user or simply login using your existing user details; new users will be asked to enter your site's URL, language, and agree to Google's terms and conditions.

When you register, you'll have to wait for Google to check that your website is considered suitable. You'll be contacted by email with Google's response. If successful, you can then create and manage adverts.

The registration process will analyze your website and provide advertising suitable to your website content.

To create and manage adverts:

1. Login to Google Adsense.

2. From **Adsense Setup**, choose **Adsense for Content**, then follow the wizard to select an ad unit, its format, corner style, and a tracking channel.

3. Copy the generated Adsense unit code snippet provided for the ad unit. You'll need this to paste into WebPlus.

To insert adverts in your web page:

1. Select a web page (or master page) on which you want to place your advert.

2. Click ⬚ **Insert Google Adsense advertisement** on the **Web Objects** toolbar's E-Commerce flyout.

3. Paste the code snippet previously copied for the unit by clicking **Paste from Clipboard**. The snippet appears in your dialog and cannot be edited.

Embed your Google Adsense advertisement

To use Google Adsense within your website, you will need an account with Google, Click on the button to sign up. | Go to Google Adsense website

Use your Google Adsense account to generate the type of advertisment you wish to display on your webpage.

Copy and Paste the Google Adsense generated code snippet into the box below:

```
<script type="text/javascript"><!--
google_ad_client = "pub-0384501779884965";|
/* 728x90, created 25/08/09 */
google_ad_slot = "5184176316";
google_ad_width = 728;
google_ad_height = 90;
//-->
</script>
<script type="text/javascript"
src="http://pagead2.googlesyndication.com/pagead/show_ads.js">
</script>
```

Paste from Clipboard | OK | Cancel

---

4. Click **OK**.

5. You'll see the mouse pointer change to the ⬚ **Paste** cursor. Position the cursor where you want to place the advert, then click to insert the advert at its original size. The advert cannot be resized.

To edit your advert:

1. Change the format and colour of your ad unit from **Adsense Setup** on the Google Adsense website, then copy the code snippet.

2. Double-click the advert on your page.

3. Paste the code snippet into the text box by clicking **Paste from Clipboard.**

4. Click **OK**.

Using lightboxes

Lightboxes are a simple way of displaying pop-up larger sized versions of pictures from thumbnails you add to your web page. If you've used the Photo Gallery feature you'll have come across this concept before. A great advantage of lightboxes is that bigger pictures can be displayed on demand and are superimposed over your web page after a gliding animation.

WebPlus also offers a simple slideshow feature (p. 104) to showcase images present on the same web page.

To create a lightbox for a picture on your web page:

1. Select the picture (preferably a thumbnail).

2. Create a hyperlink to it (click **Hyperlink...** from the **Insert** menu or right-click; see p. 85).

3. Select **Picture** from the menu, choosing a Target Window from the **Type** drop-down list of Lightbox.

4. (Optional) Click **Lightbox Options...** to add a caption to the picture in the lightbox using the **Caption** box. You can also make the picture part of a slideshow using the Slideshow drop-down list. (See Lightbox slideshows on p. 104.)

5. Click **OK**.

To restrict the display size of this linked "lightboxed" picture, WebPlus scales down outsized pictures to a maximum width and height (default 800 x 660 pixels) always preserving their aspect ratios. Images with native dimensions less than these maximum dimensions are left unchanged. The maximum width and height can be modified. (See Setting site properties on p. 32).

To create a lightbox to a local picture:

- As above but choose the **File** option instead of Picture.

You'll have the option to embed or link the picture; either way, the picture always displays using its native image dimensions.

Lightbox slideshows

Simple lightbox slideshows can be created which are based on the pictures already placed on the same web page. The lightbox itself will display controls to navigate through your slideshow.

To create a lightbox slideshow:

1. Create a lightbox for a picture on your web page (as above).

2. From the **Hyperlinks** dialog, click **Lightbox Options...**.

3. From the Lightbox Options dialog, enter a slideshow name in the **Slideshow** drop-down list. This will be used for other pictures to be added to this slideshow. Click **OK**.

4. Repeat for the next picture on the same page. The previously created slideshow name will show for other pictures. Select the slideshow name to include.

5. (Optional) Enter caption text.

6. Click **OK**.

Lightbox slideshows only apply to images on the same page. If images are added to a slideshow from different pages, then a new slideshow will be created for each page.

Lightboxes to any hyperlink target

Lightboxes are not just limited to the display of pictures. As a light box is actually a type of window, any hyperlink target can be displayed within it— typically a page in your site (e.g., a form or login page), an Internet page, blog, forum, or RSS feed. You can also view a Word file, PDF, or any other file type (using the **File** option) in your lightbox.

To create a lightbox to any hyperlink target:

1. Select an object (picture, button, or any other object).

2. Create a hyperlink to it (click **Hyperlink...** from the **Insert** menu or right-click).

3. Ensure the Target Window from the **Type** drop-down list is set to Lightbox.

4. (Optional) Click **Lightbox Options...** to set the lightbox's **Width** and **Height** dimensions.

Setting global lightbox properties

As with most settings in WebPlus, you can customize lightbox settings for the current site. Settings can be adjusted for general lightbox controls (including border type), caption controls (font, font size, font colour, opacity), and background settings (colour and opacity).

To modify lightbox properties for your site:

1. From **File>Site Properties...**, select the Lightbox menu option.

2. Modify settings in the General, Caption, and Background Settings sections.

3. (Optional) Preview your site using the **Preview Lightbox...** button, fine-tuning your settings between previews.

Inserting panels

Panels are rectangular information boxes superimposed over your web page. They host text or graphical information, or both. The ability to superimpose panels means that you can increase the amount of information available to the web visitor without altering the underlying web page content.

Panels can be made to display only when required as you click or roll over buttons, Gallery objects, or pictures. They can also be made to display permanently—great for navigation bars that never disappear on window scrolling!

Panels are versatile, and can be used for presenting:

- Showcased Events

- Sales information

- PayPal Buy Now Forms

- Useful tips and tricks

- Quick access information such as contact details and keyboard shortcuts.

- "Always-on" navigation (converted from a navigation bar; see p. 78).

- Image magnifier

To help you create professional panels, WebPlus provides an impressive selection of modern backgrounds to base your panel on. Alternatively, you can customize a background preset further or create a panel background from scratch in WebPlus's **Design Studio** (see p. 110).

Inserting your panel

To insert a panel:

1. From the **Web Objects** toolbar's Navigation flyout, click Insert Panel.

2. (Optional) From the dialog, provide an HTML ID for the panel. This can be kept as is, as the ID will always be unique.

3. From the dialog, click the panel preview box.

4. Select a preset panel type from the flyout.

5. (Optional) Drag the **Transparency** slider to set how transparent the panel appears against its background. You'll need to preview your page to see your changes.

6. Check **Align panel to browser window** to make your panel always available and fixed to a position when the web visitor scrolls the web page. Set a **Horizontal Alignment** and **Vertical Alignment** to control panel positioning.

7. (Optional) Check **Panel is initially hidden** to make the panel hidden on dialog exit. Normally, this can be left unchecked to allow to you to design your panel first.

8. Click **OK**.

9. Position the cursor where you want to place the top-left corner of your panel.

10. To insert the panel at a default size, simply click the mouse to.
    - or -
    To set the size of the panel, drag out a region instead.

Panels can be moved and resized as for any object you create in WebPlus.

To edit a panel:

- Double-click the panel and edit as described above.
  - or -

1. Select the panel.

2. From the context toolbar, select ▣ **Edit Panel**. The Panel Properties Dialog is displayed for subsequent editing.

Adding content to your panel

You should treat your panel as an empty building block which can be developed using WebPlus standard tools and features. By creating objects within the panel area, they belong to the panel. This extends to objects such as text frames, artistic text, tables, QuickShapes, and pictures. Dragging the panel around will move its associated objects.

Hiding/showing your panel

Why would you want to hide your panel once you've designed it? The power of panels comes with their ability to be hidden and then be shown as a result of rolling over or clicking a page object. This means that buttons, pictures, and gallery objects can be reveal more detailed information only when needed.

To allow this to happen, the object has to be "brought to life", i.e. an action is triggered in response to the rollover or click.

This is done by assigning an **action** and an **already created panel** to the object at the same time.

To assign an action and panel:

1. Right click the object and select **Actions...**.

2. From the dialog, click **Add...** and choose **Visibility** from the flyout.

3. Select the panel from the **Panel ID** drop-down list, then an event from the **Event** drop-down list. The event relates to the behaviour that occurs when you perform an action (i.e., when you click or rollover the object).

Panel ID:	panel_3
Event:	Show on rollover; hide on rollout

☑ Fade
Speed: △ 10

4. (Optional) A **Fade** animation of the panel is applied by default, with controllable fade **Speed**, but you can switch the animation effect off by unchecking **Fade**.

5. Click **OK**.

Finally, the panel can be hidden with a single click once you've finished designing it.

To hide a selected panel:

*   From the context toolbar, select ✳ **Hide Panel**.

The panel is replaced with a **Hidden Panel** icon. The panel is still there, and can be revealed again by disabling the Hide Panel button (by clicking). The Hide Panel option is the same as the dialog's **Panel is initially hidden** option.

On publishing your page, a rollover of the page object will display the panel.

Creating custom panel backgrounds

If you're looking to further modify your chosen background preset (or work from scratch) you can use **Design Studio**, a background design environment similar to Button Studio. This allows you to focus on your background design without the distractions of other objects on the page, i.e. the design is displayed in isolation and centred on the page.

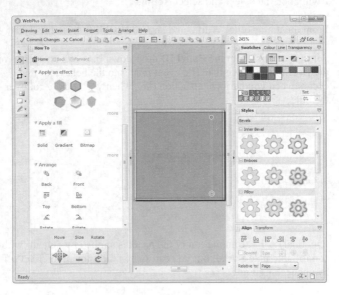

To create a custom background:

1. (Optional) From the Panel Properties dialog, select a preset from which to base your new background.

2. From the same dialog, click the ✏ **Edit** button. Design Studio is launched with your background zoomed in to fit your workspace.

3. Using standard WebPlus tools and tabs, customize your background to your liking, using the accompanying **How To tab** to interactively design your background.

4. Click **Commit Changes** on the main toolbar to exit. The modified background is updated in its original position.

The Design Studio lets you selectively prevent panel objects from scaling or stretching—**Horizontal** and **Vertical scale** flyouts on the Studio's toolbar offer absolute object control. See the How To tab for more information.

Inserting separators

Instead of designing separators as you design your custom navigation bar, you can create separators independently of navigation bars. Standalone separators are primarily used between buttons in panels previously converted from a navigation bars.

To insert a separator:

1. From the **Web Objects** toolbar's Navigation flyout, click **Insert Separator**.

2. From the dialog, click the checkboard box to reveal a set of flyout of presets.

3. Select a preset separator.

4. Click **OK**.

To create a custom separator:

1. From the above dialog, click **Edit**.

2. In **Design Studio** (see above), use standard WebPlus tools and tabs to customize your separator to your liking, using the accompanying **How To tab** to interactively design your separator.

Adding hotspots

A hotspot is a transparent hyperlink region on a web page. Usually placed on top of graphics, hotspots act like "buttons" that respond when clicked in a web browser. They are especially useful if you want the visitor to be able to click on different parts of a picture. You can draw and edit hotspots by hand, or create them to match an existing shape or region.

To draw a hotspot:

1. Click the ▨ **Insert Hotspot** button on the **Web Objects** toolbar.

2. Click and drag to draw a rectangular hotspot region. The Hyperlinks dialog appears.

3. Click to select the link destination type, and enter the specific hyperlink target (see p. 85).

4. Click **OK**. A hotspot region appears on the page.

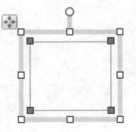

To match a hotspot to an existing shape:

1. Draw the hotspot as described above, and create the shape as described in Drawing and editing shapes on p. 303.

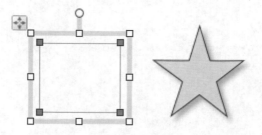

2. Select both objects and choose **Fit Hotspot to Shape** from the **Tools** menu. The hotspot region is matched to the outline of the shape. On publishing, only the shape responds to a cursor hover over.

The hotspot and shape will still be separate, so you can easily delete the shape if it's no longer needed once you've used it as a template to produce a hotspot of a desired shape.

To modify a hotspot hyperlink:

- Using the Pointer Tool, double-click the hotspot.

The Hyperlinks dialog appears with the current hotspot link target shown.

- To modify the hyperlink, select a new link destination type and/or target.

- To remove the hyperlink, change the link destination to **No Hyperlink**.

Editing hotspots

You can move and resize hotspots on the page, just like other objects. A selected hotspot has both an outer bounding box and an inner outline, which serve different purposes.

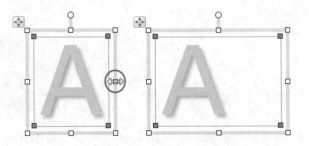

To move or resize a hotspot:

- Click to select the hotspot, then:

    - To move, click and drag from the centre, or from the hotspot's bounding box. To constrain the hotspot to vertical or horizontal movement, hold down the **Shift** key while dragging.

    - To resize, click and drag on its outer (bounding box) handles.

By editing the inner outline, you can convert rectangular hotspots into freeform shapes that closely match the parts of the underlying graphic you want to be "hot." To edit the outline, first move the mouse pointer over the hotspot's inner outline until the cursor changes to indicate whether you're over a node or a line.

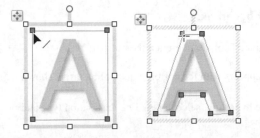

To create an extra node on a hotspot:

- Click anywhere along the hotspot's outline when you see the ▶ ╱ cursor. Drag the new node into position to modify the hotspot outline.

To change the shape of a hotspot's outline:

- Click and drag a node when you see the ⁻╎⁻ cursor.

Adding rollovers

The term **rollover** refers to an interaction between a mouse and an image. For example, you can point your mouse at a image, and see it instantly change to a different image (below). An image whose appearance changes in response to a mouse event is called a **rollover graphic**. Mouse events could typically be a hover over or mouse button press—the **state** of the graphic changes in response to these mouse events, swapping to another variant of the original image.

You can directly import rollover graphics created in Serif DrawPlus. (See online Help for more information.)

Rollover options

Adding rollovers is basically a matter of deciding which state(s) you'll want to define, then specifying an image variant for each chosen state. WebPlus provides several choices:

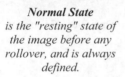

Normal State	***Over State***	***Down State***
is the "resting" state of the image before any rollover, and is always defined.	*is the state triggered by a mouseover—when the mouse pointer is directly over the image.*	*is triggered by clicking the mouse then keeping the button depressed while on the image.*

Another state, **Down+Over** (not illustrated) implies a mouseover that occurs when the image is already Down, i.e. after it's been clicked.

You can also specify a **hyperlink** event—for example, a jump to a targeted web page—that will trigger if the user releases the mouse button while in down state. And you can even group buttons on a page so they work together—and only one button in the group can be 'down' at any one time.

To create a rollover graphic:

1. In a suitable image-editing program, create the variant source images for each state you'll be defining. (See "Creating variant images" below.)

2. Click ⬚ **Insert Rollover** on the **Standard Objects** toolbar's Picture flyout.

3. Specify which rollover states (see above) you want to activate for each image by checking boxes in the Rollover Graphic dialog. For each one, use the **Browse** button to locate the corresponding source image and specify Export Options for that image (see Setting image export options on p. 265).

4. Check **Embed files in site** if you want to incorporate the image(s) in the site.

5. Check either **Normal** or **Down** as the button's initial rollover state.

6. (Optional) Click **Set...** to define a hyperlink target for the button.

7. Check **Radio button** if you want to link all the buttons (on a given page) that have this option checked, so that only one of them at a time can be down.

8. Click **OK**.

WebPlus displays the image assigned to the Normal state. It's a good idea to preview the page and test each rollover image, then return to WebPlus and revise as needed. When you preview or publish the site, WebPlus takes care of exporting one image file for each rollover state, and the HTML file for the published page incorporates the JavaScript code for the rollover event trapping.

To edit a rollover graphic:

1. Right-click (or double-click) the rollover graphic and choose **Edit Rollover...**.

2. Make new selections as needed and click **OK**.

Creating variant images

For each object with at least one activated rollover state, you'll need to provide a source image. It's the often subtle differences between the Normal image and the "variants" that make the object appear to switch from one state to another. For example, if you've checked the "Over" state for an object, you need to include a variant image that the web page can display when the button is moused over.

Adding pop-up rollovers

The most common use for pop-up rollovers in WebPlus is to hover over a picture thumbnail to show its larger representation, usually offset next to the thumbnail. The feature is simple to use and works in a similar way to the more advanced Photo Gallery. Pop-up rollovers have only two states (normal and hover over) and show the same or a different image made larger in the hover over state; compare this with WebPlus rollovers which have up to four states and only work with identically sized different "variant" images.

WebPlus lets you choose the position and size of the pop-up in relation to the "hovered over" thumbnail; even the thumbnail can be selected and resized at any time.

If captioning is required on pop-up rollovers this can be made to pop-up next to your Over image. Caption text can adopt various attributes such as font, bold/italic, size, colour.

To create a pop-up rollover:

1. Click the **Pop-Up Rollover** button on the **Standard Objects** toolbar's Picture flyout.

2. From the dialog, for the Normal rollover image click the **Browse...** button, and navigate to and select the image. Click **Open...**.

3. For the Over image, the previously chosen Normal image is used by default (typically for photo thumbnails). However, you can **Browse...** to use a completely different image.

4. (Optional) To hyperlink from the Normal image, click the **Set...** button and enter a URL. The user jumps to the hyperlink destination by clicking the image.

5. (Optional) For either image, specify **Export Options...** for that image (see Setting image export options on p. 265).

6. (Optional) Check **Embed image files in site** if you want to incorporate the image(s) in the site.

For pop-up rollovers to work effectively you'll need to position the Normal and Over images on your page. Positioning is carried out from a dedicated dialog, where each state image can be moved and resized by dragging (or by setting absolute pixel values). Each image adopts a coloured border—green for Normal state, blue for Over state.

To position rollover images:

1. In the Rollover Graphic dialog, click the **Set Rollover Position...** button at the bottom of the dialog.

2. From the dialog, select an image. The drop-down list indicates the current selection status, i.e.

   - **Normal Selection**: a Normal image is selected and shows a green border.

   - **Over Selection**: an Over image is selected showing a blue border.

   - **Caption Selection**: caption text is selected showing a red border (only shown with captioning enabled).

   If you deselect an image, the drop-down list shows **No Selection**.

3. Reposition selections by dragging and/or resize selections from corner handles (aspect ratio is always maintained when dragging). Alternatively, enter exact **Left**, **Top**, **Width**, and **Height** values in the input boxes for fine positioning. The box's down arrows offer a drop-

down list showing the last three values used for Normal, Over, and Captions (from top to bottom)—this lets you align images exactly.

4. (Optional) Check **Position relative to Normal image** to maintain the Over image's position in relation to the Normal image (when the Normal image is resized).

5. (Optional) Uncheck **Maintain aspect ratio** to allow your Normal or Over image resizing to be unconstrained. You have to then use the input boxes (not dragging) to affect unconstrained resizing.

6. Click **OK**. The Normal image will show on your page, but the Over image will only pop-up after previewing or publishing.

By building up additional Normal images as separate pop-up rollovers on your web page you can create a stylish pop-up gallery of images, with each Normal image being part of a sequence of clickable thumbnails.

To edit a pop-up rollover:

- Double-click the Normal image on the page, to display the Rollover Graphic dialog. Modify settings as appropriate.

To add captioning to Over images:

1. In the Rollover Graphic dialog, check **Display caption with Over image**.

2. Enter your caption text in the **Caption** input box.

3. Set the text attributes for the caption text using the **Font** and **Size** drop-down lists, and the **Bold** and **Italic** check boxes. For applying text colour, use the **Text Colour** drop-down gallery.

4. Check **Apply Background Colour** to enable a colour to be selected from the adjacent drop-down gallery.

5. Click **OK**.

The caption text only relates to the Over image, so to position the text next to your Over image you'll need to double-click the Normal image on your page. From the dialog, click the **Set Rollover Position...** button and reposition the text (as you would for Normal and Over images). All selected caption text shows with a red border during preview.

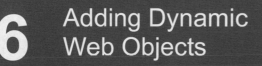

6 Adding Dynamic Web Objects

Attaching HTML code

In WebPlus, you can create pages in HTML (see Creating HTML pages on p. 59). However, WebPlus also lets you attach code to your WebPlus objects (e.g., in frames or table cells) and pages, primarily to expand the capabilities of the objects (or the page), making them more intelligent and interactive. The object or page can either dynamically generate content or can have its appearance altered within its area as a result of embedded script content.

It's not possible to edit the HTML code itself (there's no real benefit in doing so), but specific areas of the displayed code are editable for additional code to be added, i.e. clearly identifiable placeholders (text surrounded by a white highlight) will appear in your source tab's window.

```
__AddCode-"here"
```

```
<!--Header code for
```

```
<!--Preamble-->
```

```
<!--MainDivStart-->
```

```
<!--MainDivEnd-->
```

```
<!--Postamble-->
```

```
<!--Body-->
```

```
<!--Page Body Start-->
```

These are just a few of the **editable** placeholders present in the source of an HTML fragment, object or page (in fact differently named placeholders exist depending on the type of element). For example, the last placeholder shown in the list above is unique to a page's source and won't appear for an object or HTML fragment.

Any code can be inserted by cut and paste into any of the placeholder positions but typically you can include tokens, HTML code or specific scripts, e.g. JavaScript. This could be used to affect rollover behaviour on an object not otherwise possible without scripting support, e.g. an image "on-click" handler.

Adding HTML to pages

WebPlus also allows you to "view source" on a page—allowing extra **HTML code** to be added to the page. Using this approach, you can include fragments either copied from another web page, or perhaps written by yourself.

You can also import formatted HTML text from a browser or email program via the Clipboard (for example with a browser's **Select All** and **Copy** commands), using WebPlus's **File>Paste Special...** command.

Before you import your HTML code, WebPlus lets you position an HTML Code Fragment window on your page. Since you won't be able to see the effect of the HTML until you preview the site, be careful to place the window correctly. You'll definitely want to check your web page in a browser! If there's a problem, double-check the code you entered and its position on the WebPlus page (resizing if necessary). If you have some grasp of HTML, examine the page source in a text editor such as Notepad or use your browser's "View Source" mode.

To add an HTML code fragment to a page:

1. Copy the HTML code from its original source onto the Clipboard.

2. Click the <> **Insert HTML Code** button on the **Web Objects** toolbar.

3. Click on the page or pasteboard to create a new HTML Code Fragment window at a default size or drag to create a sized window.

4. In the dialog, use the **Paste to Head** or **Paste to Body** button to insert the clipboard text into the header of the file or into its body.
   - or -
   Use the scrollable code window. Enter one or more HTML code fragments into the appropriate field.

5. (Optional) If the code calls for external files, use the **Add...** button to locate them. Click the **Make Linked** button if you want to keep the file(s) separate from your site.

6. Click **OK** to close the dialog. The code will appear on your page in the HTML Code Fragment window.

Adding JavaScript

To source a vast array of JavaScript code, try searching for "javascript snippets" in your favourite search engine. You should find many thousands of sites hosting freely available code snippets. Most of these sites will clearly indicate what the JavaScript will do for you—they'll also normally let you select the JavaScript code and copy it for pasting into an HTML fragment's, object's or page's Source window, HTML table cell or directly onto the page.

Let's look at how to add some of JavaScript (sourced or written by yourself if you've experience of JavaScript programming).

To illustrate, compare the two pieces of example code below. A very simple JavaScript code snippet is added to the Source window which will display the current date on your web page. The first section of code uses the last placeholder in the above list (*<!--Page Body Start-->*), the second how the code looks after a script has replaced the placeholder.

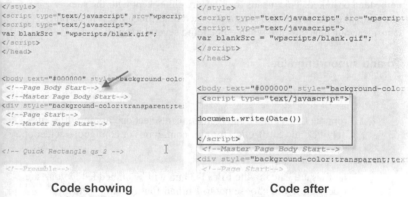

| **Code showing placeholder** | **Code after added JavaScript** |

This example illustrates where simple code is placed in a source window.

To attach code to an HTML fragment or object:

1. Select an existing HTML fragment or object.

2. From the **Format** menu, select **Attach HTML....**
    - or -
    Right-click on the object and choose the same option.

3.   In the dialog, scroll the source window to locate editable placeholders. Which placeholder you choose depends on what you want to achieve.

4.   Select all of the placeholder and paste HTML, script or any other text string to overwrite the placeholder text.
- or -
Select all of the placeholder and type directly in the placeholder's location (again overwriting the placeholder text).

5.   Click the **OK** button to return to your normal page view.

> You can make use of tokens to add a range of variables to your HTML. Use for breadcrumb navigation that will update dynamically if you add, remove or change pages within the site.

For more complex scripting, it may be necessary to add supporting files (graphics, text files, etc.) that the inserted script may use—these can be either embedded or linked. This means the files are either kept with the site (embedded) or are referenced externally via a link (much like a hyperlink). Consider your final site size when embedding several images.

To add supporting files:

1.   Click the **Add...** button.

2.   From the Open dialog, navigate to then select one or more files (use **Ctrl**-click and **Shift**-click for non-contiguous or contiguous selection, respectively). Click **Open**.

3.   The files are listed in the **Files** list and will be embedded in your site by default. If you choose not to **Embed** files (making your site smaller), then select each file and click the **Make Linked** button.

4.   Click **OK**.

At any point, you can **Add**, **Delete**, and change **Export Options** for any file.

To attach code to a page:

1.   Click 🔁 **Attach HTML to page** on the **Standard** toolbar.

2. In the dialog, scroll the window to locate editable placeholders. Which placeholder you choose depends on what you want to achieve.

3. Select all of the placeholder and paste HTML, script or any other text string to overwrite the placeholder text.
   - or -
   Select all of the placeholder and type directly in the placeholder's location (again overwriting the placeholder text).

4. To switch back to your normal page view, click the project tab at the top of the source window.

Using IDs

Objects, text columns, table rows, and table cells are always assigned a unique alphanumeric HTML ID, e.g. an ID of "qs_1",
"qs_2", etc. would be created for a new QuickShape. These IDs may be written on export to allow referencing by scripting languages in your published site. By default, they are not written on export for all objects (**globally**) but they can be exported on a **per object** basis.

To write (export) an ID (per object):

1. Right-click an object and select **ID...**.

2. In the dialog, in the **Write ID for this object** drop-down list, select "Yes".

Selecting "Use Site default" means that the setting in Site Properties is honoured—"Yes" or "No" means that the object's ID is written on export or not written irrespective of the site default setting.

To write (export) IDs (globally):

• From **File>Site Properties** (HTML Output menu option), check the appropriate check boxes for object, text column, table row, or cell.

Default HTML ID Settings

☑ Write the ID for each object
☑ Write the ID for each text column
☑ Write the ID for each table row
☑ Write the ID for each table cell

> ✎ If the object is copied on the same page or to another website, the ID number will be replaced by a new ID number.

If you need to define a custom name for your ID, you can so via the Edit Object ID dialog.

To edit the object ID name:

1. Right-click an object and select **ID...**.

2. In the dialog, modify the HTML ID value.

Tokens

WebPlus provides a range of grouped HTML annotation tokens which can be attached to HTML fragments, objects or pages. They get replaced by appropriate "real" values when you export to a file or preview your page.

Adding tokens is a simple case of inserting a token string, by copy and paste or typing directly, into one of the placeholder positions in any HTML source.

A full list of such tokens is provided in the WebPlus Help (search for tokens in the Index)

Adding forms

Web-based forms allow information to be collected from visitors to your website in an efficient and modern manner. In much the same way as traditional paper forms are used to collect information, Web-based forms offer the same form completion concepts, but take advantage of the Internet as a powerful information conduit. Some common form types include request forms, feedback forms, and guest books.

Form data can be collected in a variety of ways—by email, to a local/remote script file, or via Serif Web Resources.

Form Structure

The building blocks of a form comprise a mixture of text, graphics and form controls. Form controls are intelligent as they collect web visitor data and can be added, moved and modified in a similar way to familiar objects in WebPlus such as graphics and table elements. A control can be a button, edit box, text area, combo box, check box, radio button, CAPTCHA object, or File browser. A typical form, perhaps a email feedback form, is made up of a combination of some of these controls.

Email form

Name

Email Address

Comments

Submit   Reset

From the web visitor's perspective, information is typed into text boxes or selected from check boxes, radio buttons, or drop-down boxes. The information entered can be numeric, textual, or a mixture of both, depending on the type of field. The tab order by which fields are to be completed is configurable, as is validation of input data (see WebPlus help for more about tab order and validation).

Each field has its own set of properties relating to its appearance, its value(s), validation, or the action expected of the field.

A form's functionality only becomes active when your website is published (of course you can still preview your forms from within WebPlus, see Previewing your site on p. 337). When a web visitor enters data into, or selects a form option, the data will be sent back to a chosen destination when the form is submitted.

JavaScript can be used to allow interactivity in your web forms. It drives formatting, validation, calculations, and actions—all key functions in Web-based form development.

Where is data sent?

After submission, form data can be sent to one of the following:

- an email address (of the web developer).

- a script file (stored locally or remotely); this could write text to a text file or into a server database.

- **Serif Web Resources**; for transit of form data to your email (via Serif).

As is standard in web form management, it is possible to set the encoding type, target window/frames, submission methods (POST or GET) can be used.

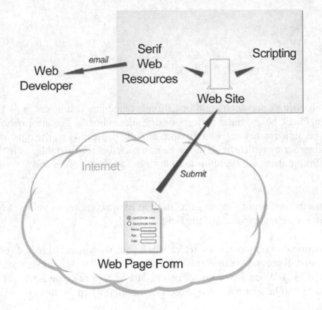

Creating forms

Contact Us

Name	
Address	
Town/City	
County	
Country	
Postcode	
Home Telephone	
Mobile	
Work Telephone	
Ext.	
Fax	
E-mail Address	

| Submit | | Reset |

Several methods exist for creating forms: you can create a pre-defined ready-to-go **standard** form (opposite), select individual form controls for your form, or create a form from scratch; the first two methods use an easy-to-use Form Wizard.

Standard forms are available for Contact information, User comments, CV submission, Opinion, and Address forms.

To create a standard form:

1. Click the ⬛ **Form Wizard** on the **Web Objects** toolbar's Form flyout.

2. In the dialog, click the **Use and adapt a standard form** icon and then **Next>**.

3. From the list of forms, select a form type while using the lower Preview pane.

   ```
   Comments 1
   Comments 2
   Contact 1
   Contact 1b
   Credit Card
   CV Submission 1
   CV Submission 2
   Opinion 1
   UK Contact Form 1
   UK Contact Form 2
   UK Contact Form 3
   ```

4. Click **Next>**.

5. In the next screen, choose to add, modify or delete controls.

- To add, click a button in the **Add** box.

- To modify a standard object, select an existing control in the window and choose **Edit Control...**. See Editing form controls on p. 136 for more information.

- To delete a standard object, select an existing control in the window and choose **Delete** (or press the **Delete** key).

- To rearrange the control order, use the 🔼 **Move Up** and 🔽 **Move Down** buttons.

6. After clicking **Next>**, choose a destination for your form data by clicking a destination button. Select **Finish** to complete the wizard.

7. ⊞ To insert the form at a default size, position the form place cursor and click the mouse.

If you're looking for design freedom, WebPlus provides a blank form and form objects from which you can design your form from scratch. You can add form controls or standard form objects, or both. See WebPlus help for more details.

To create a custom form (via Form Wizard):

1. Click the ⊞ **Form Wizard** on the **Web Objects** toolbar's Form flyout.

2. In the dialog, click the **Create a new form with the wizard** icon and then **Next>**.

3. In the next screen, you need to add form controls that will make up your form. In the Add box, either:

- For a ready-to-go form control, click the **Pre-defined** button, and pick your chosen form control. You'll need to double-click the new control in the window to name the control.
   - or -

1. Click on one of the other form controls to create from scratch.

2. In the dialog, use the internal name for the control (to uniquely identify it), or edit it and enter a label to accompany the control (this is shown on-screen). You can also edit the control by using the **Edit Control** button. Editing a control allows validation, control of form length, and other control attributes to be set. See Editing form controls on p. 136 for more information. If you've edited a value, click **OK**.

4. Repeat the above for each chosen form control as needed. They will be listed (in order of creation) in the upper window.
    Before continuing, you have to add a Submit form control to your form. This is vital to pass data to its destination. Click the **Submit Button** to automatically add the button to your form. It is normal practice to accompany this with a **Reset Button**, used to clear out form fields of data not yet submitted. Click **Next>**.

5. From the next dialog, choose a destination for your form data by clicking a destination button for email, script file (local or remote) or Serif Web Resources and a name to define the whole form. (See Submission of forms on p. 137).

6. Select **Finish** to complete the wizard.

7. To insert the form at a default size, position the form place cursor where you want the form to appear on the page, then simply click the mouse.

Form controls

Each form control is an "intelligent" object which differs from other WebPlus objects. They are intelligent because they can store visitor input and pass it on to a central location during form submission. Controls can be moved as for other objects but cannot have colours or transparency applied, borders adjusted, or resized.

A range of form controls are available from within the Form Wizard or directly from the **Web Objects** toolbar's Form flyout. You assign an internal unique name to each field and then set a variety of properties—each form control has its own set which can be modified.

Form Control Icon	Form Control Name	When to use?
OK	Form Button	Use when specifying an action that can be triggered by a button click. A whole range of buttons of varying design and function can be created.

> ✎ Submit and Reset buttons are available in the Form wizard. They perform form submission and clear all form data, respectively.

▭	Edit Box	Use for entering single-line text, numbers, or a mixture of both. Someone's surname would be a good example.
I	Text Area	Use for adding multi-line text, numbers or a mixture of both. Generally used for entering input, either textual or numerical, e.g. an enquiry, recipe, or list of figures.
▼	Combo Box	For selection from a list of items in a drop-down menu where only one item can be selected by default, e.g. a gender combo.

Female ▼
Female
Male

Combo boxes also allow for a scrollable list of items; with optional support for multiple selection. For example, to select Afghanistan, Algeria, and Andorra, use **Ctrl**-click on each item:

Afghanistan	▲
Albania	≣
Algeria	
Andorra	
Angola	
Anguilla	
Antigua and Barbuda	
Argentina	▼

You can use **Shift**-click to group select a range of items.

> When designing multiple selection combo boxes, drag the top or bottom of the Combo box to allow several items to be displayed by default.

 Check Box — Ideal when you want to select multiple items displayed side by side. A good alternative to a Combo Box if space allows. The web visitor clicks once to select or deselect the box, e.g.

☑ *Would you like to be notified of any upcoming events in the near future?*

Radio Button — Good for selection of a single mutually exclusive item from a grouped subset of choices. For example, a set of radio buttons can be used to obtain gender information from the web visitor.

Male ◉

Female ○

File Browser

Use the File browser to have your web visitors upload any file from their computers. The visitor simply navigates via a **Browse...** button and selects a local file of their choice. Some examples include uploading pictures, CVs, drawings and instructions.

CAPTCHA

Use as a security check for protecting against spamming. The form control offers a random text string for the web visitor to reproduce in a text box. Passing the check initiates form submission, which can only be via Serif Web Resources.

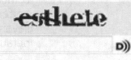

> A CAPTCHA Gateway check (p. 141) is always initiated if this control isn't present on your form. If you do use this form control, the CAPTCHA Gateway check will not be used.

Hidden objects can be added as a form control if you use the Form Wizard. Although the web visitor does not see the field, it is typically used by the web developer to ensure the data collected has an identifiable string stored with the visitor's data. An example could be a publish date relating to the web page—useful for identifying incorrectly working pages.

In addition, hidden fields can be added by right-clicking on the entire form and selecting **Edit Form Properties...**. The dialog's **Hidden Fields** tab allows for input of any number of hidden fields.

Editing form controls

Each form control type (buttons, text field, etc.) has different characteristics and therefore different values for editing. Values can be changed as you create the form or at a later time after the control has been added to the form.

The Form Wizard's **Edit Control...** button lets you modify the control during form creation. Alternatively, the control can be edited later by right-clicking on the form control on the web page and choosing the Edit option, e.g. Edit Text Box.

Submission of forms

All forms have one thing in common—they must be submitted to allow data to be collected. To do this you can either create a **Submit Button** unaided or more usually use the ready-made button in the Form Wizard. The button needs to be present on the form and is typically used with a Reset button to clear all form controls of data.

Form data submission is possible via several methods.

No action

Form data is not submitted. This option is useful if you want to temporarily disable data collection or if you haven't yet set up scripting or Serif Web Resources. At a later time you can edit the form (right-click then choose **Edit Form Properties...**) and select a valid submission method.

An email address

Use this option to bypass the usual POST/GET submission methods. When the Submit button is pressed the web visitor's default email program is launched. The form data (passcd in a single string) is added to the email body and is ready to be sent to the configured email destination. Especially useful if there is no local or remote scripting in place.

> This is an unsecure submission method—any private or confidential information will be not be encrypted.

To set up email directly:

1. With the icon enabled, add a **Form name**.

2. Enter the destination **Email address** (or select an already known email address from the drop-down menu).

A script file from my hard drive

This option is for experienced web developers with scripting expertise.

To set up a local script file:

1. With the **Script file** icon enabled, add a **Form name**.

2. Navigate to your local script file, typically a .php, .js, .cfm, .cgi, .pl, .dll, or .exe file with the **Browse...** button.

3. Check **Embed file** to include the script within the site. If unchecked, the script file will be unconnected to the site (any updates to the script will be invisible to the site).

4. Optionally, the **Export Options...** button lets you define a web file name and folder for the script.

5. Choose a submission method, encoding type, target window/frame, and Character set.

A remote script

Use if your ISP will not allow you to run your own scripts on your ISP web space. Instead, your ISP may supply a basic script file that can be linked to from your web page. Typically, the script will send the form data back to your email address (already setup with your ISP).

To set up a remote script file:

1. With the **Remote script** icon enabled, add a **Form name**.

2. Enter a URL pointing directly to a script file.

3. Choose a submission method, encoding type, target window/frame, and Character set.

Serif Web

Not everyone will have access to or even want to operate their own web server so, as an alternative to this, you can use Serif Web Resources (see p. 167). This is a free web to email gateway service which will transit valued form data

Resources

via Serif and send it to your personal email address(es)—the service does require that you firstly have a Serif Web resources login (for security reasons), which will allow you to create, edit and delete your own email destinations; these are called Form Email Targets.

To set up Serif Web Resources:

1. With the **Serif Web Resources** icon enabled, add a **Form name**.

2. Click the **Select** button (log in to Serif Web Resources if you're not already logged in).

3. From the dialog, enter your target address details:

   - Enter a target email address in the **Email Address** box.

   - Enter a **Custom subject**, the subject line string that you'll see in your web visitor's email, e.g. Email Submission from Rainbow_WWW: Contact Details.

   - Add a **Confirmation message** which will be displayed to the web visitor after they click their Submit button.

   - In the **Language** field set the language in which the confirmation message will be sent.

By creating an Edit Box form control for email addresses only, you can also send confirmation emails direct to the web visitor. You'll need to ensure that **SWR: Send confirmation email** is checked in the Edit Box properties.

Check **Reply to me** in the above dialog to make the Reply-to field of the confirmation email set to the web developer's email. This allows the visitor to contact the web developer directly via email.

4. Click **Add new**. The email entry is created and added to the Available Email Targets list. You'll notice that the entry is classed as "*Not Confirmed*". Before the service commences, you'll get a email confirmation message sent to your email address. By clicking the link, the service will be activated and the entry will change to "*Confirmed*."

5. (Optional) Repeat the above procedure to add further email targets, then select an email entry to make it active.

6. Click **OK** to exit.

The web visitor will receive a basic confirmation page generated by Serif Web Resources to acknowledge successful receipt of form data. As a useful tip you can create and assign your very own acknowledgement web page to be used instead of this basic page. Your own page is just like any other web page so you can add your own information, and design the page in the same style and appearance as the rest of your site.

To add your own acknowledgement page:

1. Right-click on the form (must submit data via Serif Web Resources) and choose **Edit Form Properties...**.

2. Switch to the Hidden Fields tab, click the **Add...** button and add the word "redirect" to the **Name** field and your intended target URL with http:// prefix (i.e., the web address of your own acknowledgement page) in the **Value** field.

3. Click **OK**. The new web page will display on the next form submission.

> No personal data will be stored on Serif web servers. All form data is redirected in real time.

CAPTCHA gateway

To protect against spam emails, Serif Web Resources uses a CAPTCHA gateway if you've not added a CAPTCHA form control directly to your form (see Form controls on p. 133). On form submission, this enables a security check offering a random text string for the web visitor to reproduce in an text box.

Passing the check initiates form submission.

RSS feeds and podcasts

Really Simple Syndication (RSS) feeds are streams of constantly changing news and information which are very popular on fast-paced websites. The popularity of RSS feeds is evident if you use Internet-based news services regularly. You'll see RSS feeds indicated on websites by a ▨ symbol—by clicking the symbol the user may be able to manually or automatically subscribe to that RSS feed via a RSS Reader.

Podcasts are syndication feeds just like RSS feeds but offer slightly different options that reflect a podcast's use of digital media such as audio and video files. Put simply, RSS feeds will publish articles, while podcasts will broadcast information as episodes.

In WebPlus, you can create your own RSS feeds or podcasts that you can frequently publish and update. In essence, you become the publisher (rather than the reader) of one or more information services containing headlines, site summaries or your very own articles. For podcasts, you broadcast media clips as episodes.

The examples below show a constantly updating fictitious school's podcast with clickable links to media (both audio and video).

Bluewood School Podcast

WW2 soldier Interview (audio)

22 September 2010, 10:59:53 | history_group@bluewood.sch.uk →

Our history group got the chance to spend some time with Arthur Peel, a WWII veteran, having served with 7th Armoured Division (aka the Desert Rats) in North Africa against Field Marshall Rommel.

🎧 Interview_soldier.mp3 *(Pending)*

SpaceZone Trip

11 September 2010, 10:51:37 | cassy@bluewood.sch.uk →

Bluewood takes to the stars in a one-day visit to the SpaceZone. Find out how Year 10 built their own rocket.

🎧 Space.mp3 *(Pending)*

Yorkminster trip (video)

09 September 2009, 10:46:24 | cassy@bluewood.sch.uk →

Year 10's trip to York to learn about the history of Yorkminster.

🎬 Yorkminster.mp4 *(Pending)*

Major's Visit (video)

07 September 2010, 10:44:14 | Paul.Chalmers@bluewood.sch.uk →

Find out how Bluewood welcomed the Major to the school. A big focus was put on the current school - community projects.

🎬 Major_visit.mp4 *(Pending)*

RSS feeds and podcasts can be configured in a very similar way in WebPlus. In fact, the process for creating your own RSS feed or podcast utilizes the same **RSS Feed Tool** within WebPlus.

If you want to reuse a third party RSS feeds/podcasts and add it to your own web page, a reader can be embedded into your web page by using the **RSS Reader Tool**.

Creating RSS feeds or podcasts

The **RSS Feed Tool** enables you to create one or more RSS feeds/podcasts from which web visitors can subscribe via their standalone feed reader, web browsers or Apple iTunes®. As you create a feed a series of settings can be applied to the feed which relate to feed title/descriptions, associated images, copyright information, categories, keywords, etc.

To insert an RSS feed or podcast:

1. Click the 📶 **RSS Feed Tool** button on the **Web Objects** toolbar's RSS flyout.

2. Click the **Add RSS Feed** or **Add Podcast** button to create a new RSS feed or podcast entry. A new feed name called **New RSS Feed** or **New Podcast** appears in the left-hand menu. With the entry selected, you'll see a list of settings for the new entry which can be modified by clicking in the Value column. Drop-down lists, dialog boxes or text input boxes let you add, select or modify values for the feed.

For example, a podcast feed and listed episodes for a school's podcasting service would look as follows:

	Name	Value

⊟ 📶 Bluewood School Podcas
  📄 Start of term - Welc
  📄 Major's Visit (video)
  📄 Yorkminster trip (vid
  📄 SpaceZone Trip
  📄 WW2 soldier Intervie
	Title	Bluewood School Podcast

	File	rss_1.xml
	Description	A school Podcasting service run by p
	URL	URL: http://www1.serifwebresource
	Image	File: C:\bluewood_media\lion crest.p
	Language Code	en-gb
	Explicit	No
	Category	
	ITunes Category	Education - Education Technology
	Blocked	No
	Author Name	Bill Stephens (IT Coordinator)
	WebMaster Email	bill.stephens@bluewood.sch.uk
	Copyright	
	Keywords	Bluewood,school,Secondary

You'll notice a series of episodes listed under the podcast feed (Bluewood School Podcast). We'll look at how to add these later.

3. Click **OK**.

4. To place the feed on the page, position the ⊹🔲 cursor and simply click the mouse.

A 📶 or 🎙 button appears at the cursor position (for an RSS feed or podcast, respectively).

💡 For one-click automatic subscription of podcasts, label your podcast symbol indicating which application the subscription will be made to.

To swap the feed for another:

- Once an RSS feed or podcast exists, double-click the feed on the page to redirect the button to another feed. Simply select a different entry and click **OK**.

  For podcasts, the dialog can also automatically subscribe the podcast to the visitor's Google Reader, My Yahoo!, or iTunes application. Pick from the **Open Podcast with** drop-down list. Otherwise, for manual subscription of RSS feeds or podcasts, the RSS Standard option is used.

Once the RSS feed or podcast is created, articles or episodes (respectively) can be added to the feed and then published. Once updated, you'll need to republish your web page (see Publishing to the web on p. 338).

To add or update articles or episodes:

1. Click the RSS Feed Tool button on the WebPlus's **Web Objects** toolbar.

2. From the RSS Feed dialog, ensure the correct feed is selected, then click the **RSS Feed Manager** button.

3. At the right of the dialog, click the **Add Article** or **Add Episode** button. This creates a new entry, provisionally titled New Article (for an RSS feed) or New Episode (for podcast) under the selected feed.

4. Edit your article/episode and its settings (see above). Drop-down lists, dialog boxes or text input boxes let you add, select or modify values for the feed.

Again, using the above school podcast example, the associated first episode could have been added with the following settings.

Name	Value
Item Title	Yorkminster trip (video)
Description	Year 10's trip to York to learn about the
Media file	File: C:\bluewood_media\2009\Yorkmins
Duration	00:22:12
Publication Date	09/09/2010 10:46:24
Explicit	No
Category	school trips
Blocked	No
Author E-mail	cassy@bluewood.sch.uk
Author Name	Cassy McDonald (Y10 head teacher)
Keywords	Yorkminster, cathedrals, history, religion
Summary	The trip was arranged so pupils can und

5. Click **OK**, then click **OK** again.

> If you're broadcasting media files stored locally, you'll be prompted
> to define the Site URL (see p. 32) during publishing. This makes
> local files accessible to visitors.

Submission of podcast feeds

For podcasts via iTunes, as a broadcaster you'll need to have your podcast
submitted to iTunes. The podcast feed has to be reviewed by iTunes staff to
check for technical problems, an acceptable login, inappropriate use of explicit
language, offensive material, and misuse of copyright material. This step means
that if your feed is approved, iTunes users will then be able to subscribe to your
podcast feed.

To submit a podcast feed to iTunes:

1. Launch iTunes.

2. Click on **Podcasts** in the LIBRARY section.

3. Select **Podcast Directory** at the bottom of the iTunes workspace.

4. From the PODCASTS QUICK LINKS box at the top-right of your
   screen, click **Submit a Podcast**.

5. In the next screen, paste your Feed URL into the **Podcast Feed URL**
   box. Your Feed URL will be a URL with an xml file name (e.g.,
   rss_1.xml) at its end.

6. Click **Continue**.

Subscribing

Subscribing to RSS feeds and Podcasts

Web visitors can subscribe to these feeds by a variety of methods.

Subscription type	Method
manual	The web visitor simply clicks on a diagnostic symbol which indicates the type of feed, i.e.

For RSS Feeds

Your published RSS feed or podcast offers a clickable subscription button, e.g.

Subscribe to this feed

This lets you add the feed to your browser's favourites.

- or -

For podcasts

Click to add your podcast to your iGoogle home page or Google Reader.

For ITunes, once a broadcaster has submitted their feed to iTunes and had it approved, the web visitor can subscribe to the podcast as follows:

1. Launch iTunes.

2. Click **Subscribe to Podcast...** from the **Advanced** menu.

3. Paste the feed's URL in the dialog's input box, then click **OK**. The podcast appears as an entry in the window. The URL can be obtained by clicking the podcast symbol and copying the resulting URL in the browser window.

automatic (podcasts only)

The web visitor clicks the 💡 icon (or associated hyperlink; see examples below). The podcast and reader is defined explicitly, so subscription is automatic. This is done by double-clicking the podcast on your page and choosing an option from the **Open Podcast with** drop-down list.

Open Podcast with:

Google Reader ▼
RSS Standard
Google Reader
My Yahoo!
iTunes

An example could be as follows:

Google Reader 💡
(One-click subscription)

My Yahoo! 💡
(One-click subscription)

ITunes 💡
(One-click subscription)

💡 Instead of a direct button, a hyperlink (see p. 85) can be created from anywhere in your site which links directly to your new feed. A special link destination type called **RSS Feed** is used.

Including third-party feeds

Instead of creating your own RSS feed or podcast you may wish to include an RSS feed from another website on your own web page—a web page's content can be boosted by inclusion of a feed from any popular news service (Reuters, BBC News, sport, etc.) or other information service (e.g., financial). Many major news and information services host lists of RSS feeds relating to specific areas of interest (geographical, **entertainment, political, music, etc.) so it's just a case of copying the link for the website's** RSS feed and pasting it into a dialog shown when clicking the WebPlus's **RSS Reader Tool**. Please bear in mind any terms and conditions in using a third-party RSS feed—these should be clearly indicated on the originating website.

The addition of the RSS feed reader to your page automatically subscribes yourself to the chosen RSS feed or podcast. There are other ways of subscribing to RSS feeds or podcasts via web browsers and iTunes, but here we'll focus on how to include the feed on your page and have it automatically receive articles or episodes.

Here's an example of a Reuters RSS newsfeed added to a WebPlus web page:

> Vestibulum semper enim non eros.
> Aliquam erat volutpat. Praesent odio nisl.
>
> ## Reuters: Top News
>
> Reuters.com is your source for breaking news, business, financial and leading global provider of news, financial information and technology individuals.
>
> 04/04/2011 10:47 PM
> **Libya rebels hope for first oil shipment**
> BENGHAZI, Libya (Reuters) - Libyan rebels hoped to begin their first in depleted by a weeks-long rebellion against Muammar Gaddafi.
> ✉ E-mail this ⚫ BOOKMARK ▦ ⊹ +
>
> 04/04/2011 10:32 PM
> **Moody's cuts Portugal, says bailout needed urgently**
> LISBON (Reuters) - Credit rating agency Moody's cut Portugal's sover government would need to seek financing support from the European
> ✉ E-mail this ⚫ BOOKMARK ▦ ⊹ +
>
> 04/04/2011 10:31 PM
> **Services PMI jumps to 13-month high in March**
> LONDON (Reuters) - The service sector activity unexpectedly logged pointing to a 0.8 percent expansion in the economy as a whole in the
> ✉ E-mail this ⚫ BOOKMARK ▦ ⊹ +

To include an RSS feed or podcast on your page:

1. Locate an RSS feed available on web pages of popular news and information services. Look for one of the following distinctive symbols, e.g.

2. Copy the Feed URL to the clipboard by right-clicking the symbol (or hyperlink) and choosing **Copy Shortcut** (Internet Explorer), **Copy Link Location** (Mozilla Firefox), or **Copy Link Address** (Google Chrome).

3. Click the 🔲 **RSS Reader Tool** button on the **Web Objects** toolbar's RSS flyout.

4. In the dialog, paste the Feed URL into the **RSS Feed URL** field.

5. (Optional) Select a different colour, font, font size, or font style for the feed's Title, Headline, or Summary Colour.

6. (Optional) Set the local time zone for your site in the **Time Zone** drop-down list.

7. (Optional) Change the **Date Format** (MM/DD or DD/MM) for the article's published date that shows in the article's header.

8. Click **OK**.

9. A ⊹ 🔲 cursor is displayed. To insert the feed in a window of default size, simply click the mouse.
   - or -
   More typically, to set the size of the feed window, drag out a region and release the mouse button.

The feed window will be filled with a peach colour with the URL shown—you'll need to publish the page to view the current new feed. Remember that the content will update automatically as the feed is updated on the original website.

For Podcasts, when the web visitor views the feed each episode can be played by clicking on the audio link, typically pointing to an MP3 file. Once downloaded and saved, the file can be played on a currently set default player (e.g., Windows Media Player).

Understanding e-commerce

E-commerce entails the buying and selling of goods on the Internet. It's difficult to escape online retailing in any Internet session these days—you've more than likely used some form of Internet shopping at some point, when buying online CDs, books, holidays, etc. Any site that supports this kind of e-commerce activity will typically make use of a shopping cart system and a payment processing system. A shopping cart is a virtual basket (think of a supermarket basket) which stores your chosen items and is used in conjunction with a payment processing system (taking the place of the supermarket's checkout).

For major companies, the shopping cart technology is developed in-house (maybe the payment processing is carried out by a third party company). For smaller companies or organizations, the shopping cart is normally a brought-in third-party solution due to the cost/resource limitations. There are many third-party shopping cart providers that can be used—all account-based and equipped to accept credit cards instead of using a traditional payment gateway (e.g., by phone).

So where does WebPlus fit into all this? Firstly, WebPlus allows you to choose one of several specially chosen shopping cart providers and, secondly, it allows you to connect to the shopping cart provider via a form or link on the WebPlus page. Forms allow for buying options (colours, quantity) to be set, as well as calculate tax rates, shipping, bulk items, etc. Links offer simple one-click purchasing without buying options. The features are provider-specific and as a result vary widely.

Configuring your shopping cart provider

A number of different shopping cart providers can be configured within WebPlus. These are the most commonly used and some, like PayPal®, you may have come across directly as an eBay® customer. The configuration process directs you to the provider's own site from where you can sign-up as a registered user.

> ✎ Use the provider's website to find out more about unique shopping cart features.

To setup a shopping cart provider:

1. Click the **Configure E-Commerce** button on the **Web Objects** toolbar's E-Commerce flyout.

2. From the **E-Commerce Configuration** dialog, you have two options depending on whether you are an existing or new user of one of the shopping cart providers, i.e.

   - If you're a new user, choose a shopping cart provider by enabling its radio button, then click the **Sign Up Now** button. The provider's web site is shown in a new browser window from where you can register with the shopping cart provider.

- If you're an existing user, enable the button next to your chosen provider, and click **Next>**. This option simply sets the default provider for your site (rather than set up a provider account).

3. The dialog is provider-specific and may show different options. As an example, choosing PayPal lets you define (via dialog) an email address to receive payments, cart handling charge, and use a "Sandbox" test tool for trying out your shopping cart before going live. Click **Next>**.

   For Sandbox testing, click the **Find Out More** button to setup a separate Sandbox login in addition to your "live" PayPal login.

4. (Optional; PayPal only) In the next dialog, check **Use the PayPal Minicart** to display a pop-up cart (as an overlay) that appears as products are added to the cart (the cart is subsequently minimized to the top-left of your browser window while items remain in your cart before checking out).

You can also configure, via the dialog, the minicart position in your browser window and edit or delete the default text displayed in the Minicart.

5. Click the **Finish** button to complete shopping cart configuration.

Once you've configured the shopping cart, you'll need to Insert an e-commerce object.

Inserting an e-commerce object (PayPal)

The creation of e-commerce objects within WebPlus takes a Wizard-based approach. An e-commerce object can be added to the web page as a form or link (i.e., a simple button) by completion of a series of dialogs. Whether you choose to use forms or links depends on the characteristics of the items you are planning to sell, and how you want to sell your goods.

For example, if you are a trader you could create an **E-Commerce button** (as a Buy Now link). This option would make an assumption about the potential transaction, i.e. that the quantity, size, style, and colour are fixed.

This is because a link is only a button and cannot host any "interactive" buying options that would be need for more complex purchases. One buyer's click will buy a standard product offering—nothing more. Useful in some situations but in others completely inadequate.

More typical purchases use **E-Commerce Forms** which offer interactive buying options such as quantity, size, etc.

Here the web visitor can choose a quantity and a size for the item.

For e-commerce scenarios, where many items are to be offered for sale, it's possible to store items for sale in a Serif database (SDB) specially structured for use with e-commerce. By adding repeating forms (or areas) on your page, the database items can be listed after database merging, and offered for sale. See Using database merge with e-commerce in online Help.

The dialog that is displayed when you add an e-commerce object will entirely depend on the currently enabled shopping cart provider (see Configuring your shopping cart provider on p. 150).

> The following procedures assume that PayPal is configured as your shopping cart.

To insert an e-commerce object:

1. Click the ⑤ **Insert an E-Commerce object** button on the **Web Objects** toolbar's E-Commerce flyout.

2. In the **Add PayPal Object** dialog, pick the email address which is to receive the payment information. WebPlus will already assume that the email address set during shopping cart configuration is used. Alternatively, uncheck the **Use the site default account** box and set a different email address to override the site default.

3. Pick an object type from the PayPal Form box. Select a "Form" radio button if you want to create an **E-Commerce Form** which will contain buying options (e.g., colour or quantity). If the product for sale has no buying options then you can use a "Link" object (i.e., to create a clickable **E-Commerce Button**). Repeating form and area options let you add items from a database rather than defining them explicitly in an Item Details dialog (see Using database merge with e-commerce in online Help). Click **Next>**.

   (Optional) If a Form or Button is not what you are looking for, enable the last option instead to paste code in a subsequent dialog. This would be code generated from PayPal's website (after login, look under Merchant Services). Click **Next>** to exit the wizard and paste the HTML code fragment onto your page.

4. In the next dialog, define a button for use. It's possible to enable a standard text button (when enabled, enter any text string) or a standard image button (when enabled, pick from an attractive selection of presets in the scrollable window). Some images support automatic rollovers.

5. Click **Next>**.

6. Item identification, pricing, tax, and weight information can be defined in the Item Details dialog.

   Options to be selected are:

   - **Item Name**: The item name for sale. Shown on the form and shopping cart.

   - **Allow customer to specify the item name**: Check to swap the above Item Name for a box in which the web visitor can enter their own item name (also good for specifying donation details).

   - **Item ID**: Add an easily identifiable string to track the item through PayPal.

   - **Currency**: Set the currency in which the transaction will be made in.

   - **Price**: The price for the item. Shown on-screen by default.

   - **Allow customer to specify the amount**: Check to swap the above Price for a box in which the web visitor can enter their own price. Use with donation forms, where the customer sets the amount.

   - **Override the tax settings..**: Check to override provider's profile's tax setting for the item. If checked, specify a flat tax rate for the item, e.g. 0% for tax-free charitable donations.

   - **Weight**: Set an item weight if you're using weight-based shipping (US only), set in your PayPal profile. Typically, pounds (lb) are used as measurement, but kilograms (kg) can also be set if needed.

Choose from the above settings and click **Next>**.

If you're using e-commerce database merging, this Item Details dialog will instead let you choose an e-commerce database for use with your chosen provider. Remember to set the currency you wish to trade in.

7.   For e-commerce forms only, two subsequent dialogs are shown:

   •   The Item Description dialog lets you optionally include an image (e.g., to preview the item for sale), and short and long descriptions that will show in the form. Click **Next>**.

   •   The Item Options dialog lets you create edit boxes, combo boxes, radio buttons, and fixed names (up to 10 options can be selected per form in PayPal; only one price-changing option) as appropriate—you can design from scratch or use previously saved options fields. Click **Next>**. Not shown for repeating forms.

8.   In the Item Details dialog, set a default quantity in the input box, or check the box to let the user specify an amount at checkout (not shown for repeating forms).
   - or -
   Set the **Add Edit box** option to let the customer define the quantity to be ordered.

   For shipping and handling associated with the order, enter a set amount for **Handling**, **Shipping**, and **Extra Shipping** charges. If left blank, the default PayPal's profile will be used instead. Not shown for repeating forms. Click **Next>**.

9.   In the Extra Customer Information dialog, choose to prompt the customer for an address, don't prompt, or require the customer to enter an address. Optionally, ask a question of the customer in the text box. Click **Next>**.

10.   The Payment Pages dialog offers some payment settings, i.e.

   •   Enter the name of your Checkout Page Style (if setup in advance via your PayPal login).

   •   Set a language for the PayPal login page. Pick for the drop-down list.

- Change the text for the Continue button on the Successful Payment Page.

- If needed, define Successful Payment Pages and/or Cancelled Payment Pages. Enter the page's URL or select an entry from the drop-down list.

11. For e-commerce forms only, choose a **form layout** from the Form Layout dialog. Several check box options let you control what gets shown on the form layout. You can disable price, and if repeating area forms are used, hide/show the item image, short/long descriptions, fixed options, and a dummy quantity edit box. Forms can be reformatted with the **Reformat form now** check box.

12. Click **Finish**.

13. To insert the form or button, position the cursor where you want it to appear on the page, then simply click the mouse.

To edit an e-commerce form or button:

1. Double-click the form or button.

2. Modify e-commerce settings screen-by-screen in the displayed dialog.

To convert to a standard form:

- Right-click on the existing e-commerce form and choose **Convert to Form**.

Using database merge

Database merge means extracting the data contents of an existing database (Serif databases .SDB, Microsoft Access, dBASE), HTML, Excel file, ODBC, or delimited text file and presenting the information—for example, into a repeating area or an HTML fragment. The contents, known as the **data source**, could be a mailing list, personnel list, product list, inventory, or sales list. In fact any information which is suitable for storage.

As well as text, it is even possible to merge **picture data** (for example, a digital photo library) into single fields or even auto-create a grid layout of pictures and text suitable for catalogs or photo albums. WebPlus can even create a photo database automatically—a simple database using the .SDB (Serif Database) format—for a set of images in a folder. You can merge images into single fields or even auto-generate a repeating layout with a grid arrangement suitable for catalogs or photo albums.

Overview

For your basic database merge needs, WebPlus provides its own **Serif Database** file format. "SDB files" as they're called (since they use the *.SDB extension) are ideal for storing unformatted, plain text data typically used for product lists, but are suitable for other tasks as well. You can build a list by creating a new SDB file and then "fill in the blanks." One advantage of using the Serif Database format is that you can edit your data (even add new fields and information) directly within WebPlus. Of course, more complex data sources have their own advantages, and WebPlus can also merge external data from a variety of other formats. You can import **plain text files** (for example, as exported from a email program), tables from **HTML** web pages, **database files** from programs such as Access, Outlook, Excel... even live **ODBC servers**!

Whatever your source of data, once you've chosen it in WebPlus you can edit the **merge list** (the actual data to be merged) by specifying which records to include or exclude, and apply advanced filtering/sorting capabilities to refine the data. You'll need to Insert placeholder fields on a placed repeating area on your web page; data will then be merged into such repeating areas. In no time, you'll be ready to Merge such that each repeating area is "regenerated" multiply within a new site with data from each record appearing in turn.

As more advanced merging features, you can use merge anchors to hyperlink between summary and main pages for each record. Additionally, merge fields can be inserted into generated page titles to allow navigation between summary lists/main pages. See Advanced database merge.

In e-commerce, it's possible to use database merging using an e-commerce Serif database and repeating Buy Now forms or repeating Add to Shopping Cart forms. Repeating areas can also be used but e-commerce forms offer transactions directly with your shopping cart provider (e.g., PayPal, Mal's, etc.) in the form of Buy Now/Add to Shopping Cart buttons. (See WebPlus Help.)

Creating a data source

You can create a new Serif Database (*.sdb) file easily within WebPlus. This database, once populated, can be used as your data source which can be merged into your web page.

To create a new Serif Database (*.sdb) file:

1. Select ⊞ **Create new database** from the Database Merge toolbar (switch on first)..

2. With "Serif Databases (*.sdb)" shown in the **Save as type** list, navigate to a folder and enter a file name for the new file, and click **Save**.

3. From the **Customize Database** dialog, click the **Insert...** button.

4. In the dialog, create each field that makes up your new database by providing a Field Name, clicking **OK** in turn.

5. The fields are displayed in the Customize Database dialog:

   - To delete a field, select the field name and click **Delete**.

- To Rename a field, select the field name and click **Rename...**

- To change the order of fields within the list, select the field name and click **Move Up** or **Move Down**.

6. Click **OK**.

7. The Edit Database dialog appears, displaying the first record with six fields in view. Scroll down to view additional fields if created. Since it's a new database, the fields will be blank; you can start entering information now (i.e., add a record), or wait until later. To enter information, simply type into a field. To create a new record, click **Add** then repeat for each record then once finished, click **OK**.

8. Click **OK** to close the Merge List dialog and return to the site.

> WebPlus lets you create your own photo databases for showcasing digital art—EXIF data is also stored. See WebPlus help for more details.

Inserting repeating areas for your data

For merging to work correctly you'll need to include the contents of your data source on a web page. WebPlus assists by allowing you to quickly create a **repeating layout** that arranges placeholder fields, generating a new site with as many pages as needed and populating the fields with text or images from a specified data source. You can create any number of data sources, but can only have one open at a time per repeating area.

> Each repeating area has its own data source; only one repeating area can occupy each web page.

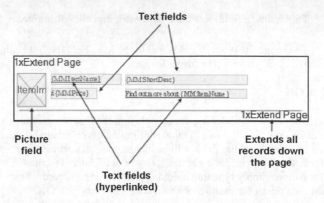

Text fields

Picture field

Text fields (hyperlinked)

Extends all records down the page

A repeating layout starts with a **repeating area**—basically a single cell whose unit size determines how many database records can tile across and down on a page. Within the repeating area, you can place any elements, such as:

- One or more **text fields** with data drawn from the same record.

- One or more **picture fields** where you want merged picture(s) from a particular data record to appear.

- Other objects such as artistic text, QuickShapes... anything you want!

You take care of creating the repeating area and placing the fields (or other elements), while WebPlus takes care of replicating them into a repeating grid layout and merging text or pictures from your data source into a new site. Each repeating area is "regenerated" multiply within the new site, with data from a different record appearing in turn.

To create a repeating layout:

1. Choose any suitable data source.

2. Click the ![icon] **Insert Repeating Area** button on the **Database Merge** toolbar (switch on first).

3. From the Choose merge database dialog, click **Browse...** to select a data source, click **Open**, then click **OK**. You can also create a new database at this point by clicking **New...** (see Creating a data source above).

4. The **Repeating Area Tile Setup** dialog appears, showing a page layout that initially consists of a 1x4 tiling grid: one repeating area across the page, and four down. The preview region at the left reflects the current dialog settings.

5. You can either set precise properties for the repeating area (the basic unit) in the dialog, or close the dialog and use direct dragging to establish the area's size and shape. Or you can use a combined approach, reopening the dialog as often as needed.

- Using the dialog, specify the grid **Layout** as the number of repeating areas you want to appear **Across** and **Down**. Other settings you can change include the **Left** and **Top Position** on the page, the repeating area's **Width** and **Height**, and optional horizontal or vertical **Gaps** between repeating areas. Check **Extend page to fit all tiles** to have all records shown on a single page (especially recommended for single-line summary lists)—the Down layout option is ignored.

- On the page, you can drag the repeating area object to move it, or drag a handle to resize it.

When you save a site, WebPlus "remembers" the current data source and reopens it "behind the scenes" automatically the next time you open the web page—so as long as you're using the same source, you won't need to reopen it yourself.

To edit an existing repeating layout:

1. With repeating area selected, click ⬚ **Repeating Area Layout** on the context toolbar.

2. The Repeating Area Tile Setup dialog appears, which lets you modify the repeating area layout.

Opening a different data source

As well as creating a Serif database file, WebPlus will also let you open a different already existing Serif database file or other external data source such as plain text file (comma-delimited or fixed-width), other database, spreadsheet, and more. You can edit, select, filter, and/or sort the actual data to be merged.

To open a different data source:

1. With repeating area selected, click ⬚ **Edit database** on the context toolbar.

2. In the dialog, click the **Browse...** button and from the down arrow on the file format drop-down list adjacent to the **File name** drop-down list, select the type of data source you want to open, and click **Open**.

   Depending on the type of data source, follow any additional instructions provided by WebPlus. For example:

   - **If the data source includes more than one table**: You'll be prompted to specify which table to import.

   - **If you selected a text file** (.TXT, .CSV, .TAB, .ASC) with source data in delimited or fixed-width format: WebPlus displays a Data Format dialog, with a preview of the selected file's data.

     - On the first screen, specify either **Delimited** or **Fixed Width**. If the first data record lists the titles of the various columns, check **First Line Contains Column Headers**. If your source file uses a **Text Qualifier** (for example, a quote mark to surround text fields like "Apt 3, 14 Hopalong Crescent" that might contain commas or otherwise be read as multiple fields), select the appropriate character in the list.

     - Click **Next**. The appearance of the next screen depends on whether you've specified a delimited or fixed-width file. You can either specify the delimiter or check (and correct, if necessary) the breaks used to separate the data fields. Double-check that the data preview appears correct, then click **Finish**.
       Note: Should you need to reformat the data once you've closed the wizard, simply reopen the source file and run through the Data Format dialog again, changing settings as needed.

3. Once you've completed any intermediate steps, the Choose merge database dialog appears. If you click the **Edit...** button, the Merge List dialog appears, presenting the data in row/column format and allowing you to select, filter, and/or sort the actual data to be merged. You can make any necessary changes now or later.

4. Click **OK** to close the Merge List dialog and return to the web page. The data source you've just opened remains the active data source.

Editing Serif Database files

Each record in a Serif Database (*.sdb) file contains 20 standard fields. For data stored in SDB format, you can use the Edit Database dialog to create or delete records, enter information, find occurrences of specific text, or revise the field order—even add new fields and data.

Other database files are not editable.

To edit a Serif Database (*.sdb) file:

1. With repeating area selected, click 🖼 **Edit database** on the context toolbar.

2. In the dialog, click the **Edit...** button. (If the button is disabled, the current data source is not an SDB file.)

3. The Merge List dialog appears, presenting the data in row/column format and allows you to edit, select, filter, and/or sort the actual data to be merged. You can make any necessary changes now or later. Click the **Edit...** button.

4. The first record of the current database appears, with six fields in view (scroll down to view additional fields). Use the Edit Database dialog to edit the data.

   - To enter information, simply type into a field. Each field is limited to a maximum of 255 characters.

   - To create a new record, click **Add**.

   - Use the arrow buttons to navigate between records, or type in a record number and press **Enter**.

   - To delete the current record, click **Delete**. If you click **Delete** on the first record, its information is cleared, but the record form remains.

- To find occurrences of specific text, click **Find...** and specify the **Field** to be searched. The Record list displays any text appearing in that field throughout the database. Double-click an entry (or select it and click **OK**), to view that particular record.

- To customize the database fields, click **Customize...**. In the dialog, click **Insert...** to create a new field, or select a field and click **Delete** to remove one. To rename a field, select it and click **Rename...**. You can also click **Move Up** or **Move Down** to change the order of fields within the list.

5. To update the list and dismiss the dialog, click **OK**.

Closing the Edit Database dialog does not close the database file; it remains the active data source for database merge purposes. However, any changes you've made are saved to disk at this time.

Inserting placeholders for your data

In order to merge information from a structured data source into a web page, you need to insert **placeholder fields** into your created repeating area (see above) so WebPlus knows which fields' data to use. There are actually two kinds of placeholders. **Text fields** obviously handle text-based information like address list data; picture fields will add images retrieved from stored file path names in your database.

To insert a text or picture field placeholder:

1. With repeating area selected, click the 🔲 **Insert Text Field** or 🔲 **Insert Picture Field** button on the context toolbar.

   A dialog appears, displaying a list of fields (text or picture) in the currently selected data source.

2. From the scrolling list in the dialog, double-click the field to insert (or select it and click **Insert**).

3. The field appears on your web page. The dialog remains open so you can insert additional fields if needed.

4. Drag each field so that it is placed exactly within your repeating area—resize if necessary. There's a subtle "locking moment" (with

Snapping either on or off) when the field attaches to the repeat area. The field's contents turn shaded and subsequently, dragging the repeating area object also drags its contents.

For picture fields, set display properties such as picture size and alignment within the picture field, right-click the field and choose **Frame Properties....** Typically, the **Scale to Minimum Fit** option works best for Picture fields. You can also resize the frame itself by dragging its handles.

5. To dismiss the dialog, click **Close**.

Selecting, filtering, and sorting the merge list

Whatever kind of data source you're using, at any time you can view the current data in row/column format, with the option of customizing the **merge list** (the actual data to be merged) by including or excluding specific records. You can do this "by hand" or preferably by applying powerful filtering and sorting options that let you include just certain records, or arrange records in order, based on the contents of specific fields. For example, with an address list or contact database you could sort by postal code and then by last name.

To edit the current merge list:

1. With repeating area selected, click   **Edit database** on the context toolbar.

2. Use the **Edit...** button to access the Merge List dialog.

3. Specify which records to include or exclude (by checking/unchecking), and apply advanced filtering/sorting capabilities (via **Filter...** button) to refine the data.

4. Click **OK**.

Merging and publishing

Once you've selected which records to merge (your **merge list**) and inserted all necessary placeholders as detailed above, you're ready to merge your database content to a temporary site, and then publish.

To merge to a new site:

1. Click **Merge to New Site** on the context toolbar.

2. WebPlus now generates a new site in a separate window, replicating the basic repeating area as many times as there are records in the data. The layout uses the grid arrangement you specified, with each unique cell including data from a single record, following the order of records in the merge list. WebPlus inserts new pages as needed to include all the records. Note that the repeating area is no longer present; it's been converted to a grid layout using merged data rather than placeholder fields.

> Should you need to adjust display properties such as picture size and alignment for any individual picture frame, right-click the frame and choose **Frame Properties...**.

The original site remains open in its own window. Don't forget to save it in case you need to repeat the merge process with another data set! If you're not happy with the resulting site, simply return to the original, make adjustments, and repeat the merge process.

To publish your site:

With your merged site currently active, choose **Publish Site>** on the **File** menu and select Publish to Web.

> By default, merging will take place automatically before you publish; if you don't want to merge each time, uncheck **Merge before publishing** in the Publish to Web dialog.

Using Smart objects

For modern interactive web features (counters, forums, blogs, resource booking, and more), WebPlus uses server-sided **Smart objects** placed on the page. Smart objects store gathered web visitor data on Serif's own secure server space. These objects are available from **Serif Web Resources**, a secure online service for not just creating and inserting smart objects, but for storing and managing object data once your site is published and live.

Let's look at each Smart object you'll find in Web Resources and what you can do with them.

Name	Use
Active Viewers	Use to show how many people are currently viewing the web page.
Blog	A blog acts as a personal journal on your web page which hosts your own published articles in an easy-to-use text editor. Articles can be commented on by visitors to the web page. With blogs you can:

- Add your own personal **profile**.

- Add **social bookmarking links**.

- Use article **trackbacks** for inter-blog cross-referencing; use receive trackbacks.

- Use **tagging** to categorize articles for easier user access.

- Enable users to subscribe to articles (most recent articles/comments) via RSS feed readers.

- Enable CAPTCHA anti-spam protection.

- Apply a **Visual Styles** (theme) to your blog.

- Use **Editor groups** for multi-author article publishing (see p. 184).

Forum

Add a thread-based discussion forum to your site, optionally in a full-sized window. With forums you can:

- Under different **categories** (e.g., Motoring) add multiple **subforums** (Classics, Convertibles, Custom, etc.).

- Establish **access control** for users and moderators (see p. 184).

- Set forum **privacy** as publicly readable or private.

- Apply a **theme** (style) to the overall forum object.

- Create, edit, and assign **user ranks**.

- Set **user permissions**.

Users can view number of topics, posts, and last post submitted, and obviously post to the forum.

Hit Counter

A straightforward count of the number of hits on the current page (reset as needed). Different styles can be adopted.

News

Add a news window onto your page. The object supports RTF editing as well as paragraph styles, hyperlinks, inserted media, and even HTML source editing.

Poll

Set up an online poll to canvass web visitor's opinions.

Content Management System (CMS)

Lets the web developer add content to web pages remotely without accessing and publishing via WebPlus. Content is article-based where articles can be categorized, created, edited, deleted and arranged into categories. Site visitors can comment on and rate any article.

Your CMS can be given its own colours.

Resource Booker

Host the online booking of hotel rooms, meeting rooms, rehearsal rooms, theatre tickets, and more. Book by the hour or by the day, as recurring bookings, and with pricing options for different age groups.

Shout Box

Acts as an interactive chat window similar to Windows Messenger. Let your web visitors chat amongst themselves.

User List

The User List Smart object operates in two modes (each mode selectable via a pop-up dialog):

- **Mailing List mode**: Have website visitors sign up to newsletters, party confirmations, information request, and many more. Lists can be controlled manually or by self-subscription.

- **Access Control mode**: Control accessibility to pages, forums, blogs, and CMS by using user groups. See Access Control on p. 176 for more details.

  - Enable CAPTCHA anti-spam protection during user registration.

  - Create user groups (with optional user sign-up, auto-login, and connection to Smart objects).

  - Add, remove, suspend, or ban users.

> As Smart Objects are stored in Serif Web Resources, you can use Help buttons accompanying each Smart Object (as you create and manage them) for more detailed information.

For security reasons, the objects are only available via a **Serif Web Resources** login accessible from within WebPlus. If you don't have a valid username and password you must create a Web Resources account first.

- If your email address is already known to Serif (maybe you've just registered or have registered previously) you'll be asked for a limited number of questions to complete account registration.

- If you're new to Serif and unregistered you'll have to complete full security as required. Full instructions are provided on login screens.

To create a Serif Web Resources account:

1. Click **Smart Object Tool** on the **Web Objects** toolbar.

2. In the login dialog, click the **Create Account** link under the login boxes.

3. In the next dialog, enter your current email address, screen name, and a password twice. You'll need to review and agree to Serif's terms and conditions of use (via a check box).

4. Click the **Signup** button.

5. An additional dialog, will ask for personal details, plus a few check boxes if you would like to receive the Serif Community newsletter, Serif offers, and/or other third-party offers.

6. A confirmation email will be sent to your email address. Click the link in the email and you're ready to login to Serif Web Resources (by clicking the Smart Object Tool again).

To clear Account details:

- Go to **Tools>Options** and click **Clear Account Details** shown from the **Options>General** menu option. This will clear the stored login details for Serif Web Resources so that automatic login will no longer work. Details will need to be entered next time so be sure you've remembered your password.

To access Web Resources:

1. Click **Smart Object Tool** on the **Web Objects** toolbar.

2. At the login prompt enter your username and your password. Check **Remember account details** to access Web Resources directly in future (bypassing the login screen).

3. Click the **Login** button. The Smart Objects dialog is displayed.

Once created, you can check your account details from the Smart Objects dialog by clicking the **My Account** button.

Creating Smart objects

Think of a Smart object as being a general term for elements that you'll use on your page—as discussed previously. Smart objects are not added directly to the page from Serif Web Resources, but are first added to your own object library (the library lets you manage and edit each object)—objects can then be added to the web page immediately or at a later date.

> Some Smart objects are conditional on another Smart object being created first. An example is the Forum Smart Object which requires the User List smart object to be created first.

Smart objects can be organized into categorized **profiles**. These are useful if you're managing multiple websites, where smart objects can be grouped together under a profile per site.

To create Smart object profiles:

1. From the main Smart Objects dialog, click the **Manage Profiles** button at the bottom of the My Smart Objects Library pane.

2. Click **New profile**, then enter a new **Name** in the text box.

3. Click **Save**, then click **Exit**.

The profile is added to the top of the My Smart Object Library pane. You can then add existing Smart objects into your new profile by drag and drop.

To add an object to the library:

1. From the main Smart Objects dialog, click the **New...** button.

2. In the **Create Smart Object** dialog, use the scroll bar to navigate the list, then select a Smart object.

3. (Optional) For your Smart object to operate in a language other than English, select from the **Language** drop-down menu.

4. Select **OK**. Depending on the type of object selected, a different Create dialog will be displayed showing options specific to the Smart object.

5. From the dialog:

- Enter your own **Name** for the object.

- (Optional) Select a **Profile** from the drop-down menu if created previously.

- (Optional) A **Filter Offsite** string (access to the object will be restricted to the domain entered and will prevent the URL from being copied).

- (Optional) Change the object specific settings, e.g. for some objects you can also set the titling, colours (for body, text and border), and border thickness if appropriate.

6. Click **Create**.

The named object will be shown in a list in the My Smart Objects Library left-hand pane. Here's an example of a selection of Smart objects, some grouped under a custom profile named Rainbow WWW Objects.

All Smart objects can be added to the page, but some Smart object types (i.e., forums or blogs) are not added to a web page but instead access Serif Web Resources directly (via offsite links or hyperlinks; see p. 55 or p. 85, respectively). The main advantage is that there is no constraint by having the Smart object contained within your page dimensions (avoiding window scrolling).

To add a Smart object to your web page:

1. From the Smart Objects dialog, select the chosen object from the left-hand pane and click the **Insert** button.

2. ⊹ To insert the object at a default size, position the cursor where you want the object to appear on the page, then simply click the mouse.

The Smart object will automatically preview on the page so you'll get a good feel for how your published Smart object will look.

Editing Smart objects

Once an object is created it can be edited either in the My Smart Object Library or directly on the page. Typically, you might want to alter the appearance of the object from its original settings, maybe change a Poll question, or reset a Hit Counter back to zero.

Editing an object only affects the object itself and does not alter any collected data.

The dialog options for editing and creating a Smart object are identical.

To edit a Smart object in your library:

*   From the Smart Objects dialog, click the **Edit...** button at the bottom of the My Smart Objects Library pane.

To edit a Smart object on your page:

*   Double-click the object to reveal the object's Edit dialog.

🖎   If you edit an object on the web page the change is also reflected in the Objects library and vice versa.

Applying Smart Object colours

You can make colour changes specifically to your Blog, Forum, or CMS as you edit or manage them. Each Smart Object type has its own colour settings, i.e.

Smart Object	How to Configure colour
Blog	**Visual Style** drop-down list in **Edit - New Blog** dialog.
Forum	**Forum Themes** drop-down list in **Manage - My Forum** dialog.
CMS	**Title**, **Body**, and **Info** buttons from **Edit - New CMS** dialog.

In addition to these colour settings you can override your Smart Object's **text** and **hyperlink colours** to match those used by text and hyperlinks in your site. In doing so your Smart Objects will fit seamlessly with the look and feel of your site. By default, your site's current scheme's text and hyperlink colours are used on override.

To override Smart Object's text and hyperlink colours:

1. From the **File** menu, select **Site Properties...**.

2. From the dialog, select **Features**.

3. Check **Override colours in Smart Objects**.

Leaving the Text and Hyperlinks drop-down lists unchanged will use the currently set scheme colours
(indicated by numbers). However, you can select alternative schemed or non-schemed colours instead.

Managing Smart objects

While editing Smart objects affects how the object operates, managing Smart objects can be used to manage the object's "gathered" data when the web page is published. Some Smart objects such as Hit Counters don't need to be managed as they just increment on each web visit (you can reset the counters though). However, other more complex Smart objects, such as Forum, Blog, Resource Booker, User List, Poll, and Shout Box store collected visitor data such as article comments, email addresses, poll results, and a chat messaging log.

The CMS Smart object can only be managed via a web browser using the URL www.serifwebresources.com.

To manage a Smart object from your library:

- From the Smart Objects dialog, click the **Manage** button at the bottom of the My Smart Objects Library pane. The management options differ for each Smart object type.

See online Help for an overview of management functions.

To manage Smart objects directly over the Internet:

- Login to www.serifwebresources.com to control all your Smart objects independently of your WebPlus site. Use your usual Web Resources login as before.

Deleting Smart objects

To delete an object from the library:

- Select the object's entry in the My Smart Objects Library pane and click the **Delete** button. A confirmation message is displayed.

This will cause any uploaded web page which includes the object to display an empty space until the object is removed from the corresponding WebPlus's web page and the web page uploaded again.

To delete an object on your page:

- Select the object and press the **Delete** key.

Access control

Access control lets you apply security to your site, either to restrict access to specific pages or to control user access to forums, blogs, and CMS.

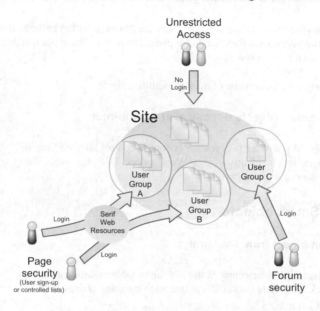

- **For page security**: login to a password-protected page(s) or via an on-the-page login box. Typically of use in personal websites or small enterprise websites, you can allow free access to most of your site, with only a limited set of pages accessible to selected web visitors. As an example, a Photo Gallery page of your family can be made "private" but still be shared with your relatives (under password control). The login details are stored in a user group associated with the page which contains a list of authorized users; the users are added manually by the site manager or new users can self-register.

- **For Smart object security**: provides access control for forums, blogs, and CMS (see p. 184).

  - Forums: for management of users and group moderation.

  - Blogs: for adding and removing articles via an Editors group.

  - CMS: for managing articles in your CMS.

Access control is possible via Serif Web Resources (p. 167) by using a **User List** Smart object, which can be created to manage user groups and users, and how users sign in.

Successful establishment of access control on your website, is dependent on following the steps below.

- Setting up your User List Smart object

- Adding users (manual or self-registration)

- Enabling access control

- Adding a login box

- Advanced user control

Setting up your User List Smart object

You'll need to firstly create a User List Smart object then create one or more groups connected to that Smart object. Normally, you'll just need one Smart object per site—the individual groups can then be used to control access to specific pages or Smart object resources.

To create a User List smart object:

1. Click the **Smart Object Tool** button on the **Web Objects** toolbar.

2. Login to Serif Web Resources (See Using Smart objects; p. 167). This assumes you have a valid login; otherwise you will have to register.

3. From the dialog, select the **New...** button at the bottom of the My Smart objects Library pane.

4. In the dialog, use the scroll bar to navigate the list of Smart objects, then select **User List**, then click **OK**.

5. From the pop-up dialog, select **Access Control**.

6. From the dialog, name your Smart object, save it in a profile, and modify colours and fonts for title, text/labels, buttons, or border.

7. Click **Create**. Your new Smart object is listed in your Smart objects Library, e.g.

Rainbow_WWW
(User List - Access Control Mode)

8. Click **Exit** to logout of Serif Web Resources.

Once you've created your Smart object, you can create and associate user groups to it using the Manage feature.

To control user signup and security:

1. Click **Smart Object Tool** on the **Web Objects** toolbar.

2. With your User List Smart object selected, in the My Smart Objects Library pane, click the **Manage** button to reveal the Users dialog.

3. To switch on self-registration user sign up to the Smart object, check **Enable signups to User List**. This allows a Sign up link to be shown on a placed login box.

4. For extra security at user sign in, check **CAPTCHA enabled**. CAPTCHA is an anti-spamming technique where arbitrary server-generated text is displayed; the web visitor enters the text for subsequent validation.

5. Enter a redirect URL in the **Redirect after login** box if you want to direct the user to a specific web page after successful login.

6. Click **Update**.

To create a user group:

1. From the dialog, click **Groups** from the top menu.

| Users | Groups | Import/Export | Bans |

2. From the Create New Group dialog, enter a **Group Name**; this should reflect how the group is intended to be used, e.g. "Photoaccess".

Create New Group

Group Name: Photoaccess

Add new users on signup: ☐   Automatic login/logout: ☐

3. Click the **Create Group** button, verify dialog settings, then click **Done**. The group will be added to the **Group** drop-down menu.

To manage a user group:

- Select the group name from the **Group** drop-down menu, then click **Manage Group**.

From the dialog, you can rename the group and display the number of group users. You can make changes by clicking the **Update Group** button, or remove the group with the **Delete Group** button.

Adding users (manual or self-registration)

Adding users manually

Typically, adding users manually is great for controlled environments such as small businesses, organizations, or clubs where users are "known."

For each user group that is created, a group of **users** can be added to each user group by manual entry or import from a comma-delimited text file by the web manager.

It's possible to use either one user login (everyone uses the same login) or create a login per user for more user control (e.g., for membership lists).

Self-registration user sign up

Conversely, user sign up is intended for more public access where controlling users is impractical—the user can simply register then sign in using their login credentials. The web manager still has the option to manage those users within their groups via the User List Smart object. This method requires an on-screen login box to be placed on the page (normally a master page).

You can add more than one user to the same user group. The same user can belong to multiple user groups.

To add a user manually:

1. Click the ⬚ **Smart Object Tool** button on the **Web Objects** toolbar.

2. With your User List Smart object selected in the My Smart objects Library pane, click the object's **Manage** button to reveal the Users dialog.

3. From the **Add New User** section at the bottom of the dialog, enter the user's email address in the **Email** box.

    Email: blaker@lameduck.com

    ☑ Require activation

    ☑ Email User
    Note: If you uncheck this box, you must

    [Add User]

    With **Require activation** checked, an activation link will be emailed to the user along with an auto-generated password. When unchecked, only an auto-generated password will be emailed.

    With **Email User** checked, an email will be sent to the user; if unchecked, no email is sent but the user is added. The password needs to be communicated to the user via other means (telephone or verbally).

4. Click the **Add User** button. The user is added to the user list in the **Users** section.

5. To assign users to a group, click **Groups** from the top menu.

    | Users | Groups | Import/Export | Bans |

6. Select the group from the **Group** drop-down list, then add the selected user from the Users box to the Group box by clicking the **Add** button (if adding all users, click **Add All**). The user will now belong to the user group. To remove, use the **Remove** (or **Remove All**) buttons from the group.

If configured, you can make users sign up by themselves, avoiding the need to manually add and manage every user as described above. This is done via Serif Web Resources.

To enable self-registration user sign up:

> This method requires a login box to be added to the master page. A new visitor to the site can click the Sign up link on the login box.

1. Click ![icon] **Smart Object Tool** on the **Web Objects** toolbar.

2. With your User List Smart object selected in the My Smart objects Library pane, click the object's **Manage** button.

3. From the Users dialog, click Groups from the top menu.

Users	Groups	Import/Export	Bans

4. From the dialog, select an existing group from the **Group** drop-down list, and click **Manage Group**.

5. Check **Add new users on signup**—the user's login details on sign up will be added to the user group during registration. When checked, the sign in process allows access to **all** groups that are "sign up enabled", otherwise restricted pages will be protected.

6. Click **Update Group** and then **Done**.

Enabling access control

To enable access control on your web page:

1. With the web page currently in view, click 🔒 **Page Security** on the Default context toolbar.

2. Check **Protect page with password** to enable access control. You'll notice that the **Change/Manage** button becomes active. Click this button to reveal currently available user groups (in bold) and the User List Smart object to which they belong.

> **Photoaccess**
> Rainbow_WWW
>
> **Internal**
> Rainbow_WWW
>
> **Forum_access**
> Rainbow_WWW
>
> **Forum_access**
> Outreach_WWW

3. From the User Groups dialog, select the user group, e.g. Photoaccess, then click **OK**. Your page's Page Security tab should show that the page is password protected and that the user group has been assigned.

> Page Security Settings
>
> ☑ Protect page with password
>
> Current User Group: Photoaccess
>
> [Change / Manage]

4. Click **OK**, then **OK** again to exit the dialogs.

🔦 You'll now notice the page in the Site tab showing a 🔑 key symbol which indicates that page security is set.

Adding a login box

WebPlus lets you add a login/logout input box onto a page in your website. This means that a registered web visitor can gain access to any restricted pages by signing in to the site.

The login box is actually a visual representation of the User List Smart object; it is placed on the page as well as existing just in Serif Web Resources.

Users can be added manually in Serif Web Resources or via self-registration user sign up.

> ✎ Add the login box to the site's master page. Any web page using the master page will then offer the user the opportunity to sign in to the website.

To add a user login box:

1. Follow the procedure under Enabling access control (see p. 182) but instead of exiting the dialog, pick a page to place your login box, then click the **Insert** button.

2. Position the **Paste** cursor where you want the user login box, then click the mouse to insert the object at a default size.

3. Enable self-registration user sign up as described previously (see p. 181).

Advanced user control

Some additional features allow you to import/export, suspend, and ban/unban users within user groups. A banned user is banned globally (access to all User Groups is prevented).

See online Help for more details.

Access control with forums, blogs, and CMS

To set up access control for forums:

1. Select the already created User List Smart object for access control
    when creating a forum.

Forum Name

Name
Golf Forum

Profile
Rainbow WWW Objects ▾

☑ Preview colours

Filter Offsite

Forum Description
Write about your best go

Access Control
Rainbow_WWW genei ▾
Rainbow_WWW general

Time Zone
GMT ▾

WebPlus will automatically create a user group, also called Golf
Forum, to allow self-registration user sign up and sign in. The forum
visitor will need to click the register link and sign up.

2. To set up a forum Moderator group, you'll need to create a moderator
    group, add moderators manually, manage the forum, and choose the
    group from the **Moderated by Group** drop-down menu.

To set up access control for blogs or CMS:

You'll need to create an Editors group, add Editors manually, then either:

*   For blogs, click **Manage** and choose the group from the **Editors
    Group** drop-down menu.
    - or -

    For CMS, click Manage and choose Permissions once directed to
    www.serifwebresources.com. The same menu is offered as above.

Working with Text

Importing text from a file

Importing text from a word-processor file is a quick way to build up text content for your site (but you can also create a story using WritePlus). If you use your current word processor (such as Microsoft Word) to create the text files for your site, you can import any number of files into one site.

As well as the WritePlus format (.stt), a range of popular word processing and text formats can be imported, including:

ANSI text	.txt
Microsoft Word 2007/2010	.docx/.dotx
Microsoft Word 2000/2003	.doc/.dot
MS Works	.wps
Open Office text	.odt
Rich Text Format	.rtf
Wordperfect	.wpd
Write	.wri

For Microsoft Word formats created in any Windows operating system you don't need to have Microsoft Word installed locally. This means you can reuse third-party text content in WebPlus without the supporting application.

WebPlus will import text into either a new creative text frame (supports text flow between frames) or into a selected HTML or creative text frame (HTML frames do not support text flow) already on your web page. See Understanding text frames on p. 188 for more information.

> WebPlus will preserve the formatting of imported word-processor text. However, if you're using your word processor to create text specifically for WebPlus, you'll save time by typing as text only, and applying formatting later in WebPlus.

✎ Tables cannot be imported.

To import text from a file:

1. (Optional) If using an existing empty text frame, select the frame. If inserting text into a populated text frame, click for an insertion point (or select a portion of text to be replaced).

2. Choose **Text File...** from the **Insert** menu.

3. From the **Open** dialog, select the format of the source file to be imported and locate the file itself.

4. Check the **Retain Format** box to retain the source file's formatting styles. Uncheck the box to discard this information. In either case, WebPlus will preserve basic character properties like italic, bold, and underline, and paragraph properties like alignment (left, centre, right, justified).

5. Click **Open**.

The text will be imported into the pre-selected text object or a new text frame. For HTML frames, the text may overflow your frame. To resolve this, see Controlling overflowing frame text on p. 191.

For Creative frames, if all of the imported text cannot fit into the active text frame you'll be prompted via dialog to either create extra frames to accommodate overflow text (click **Yes**) or place the overflow text in a hidden overflow area (click **No**).

Understanding text frames

Typically, text in WebPlus goes into **HTML text frames**, which work equally well as containers for single words or standalone paragraphs and articles. You can also use **artistic text** for standalone text with special effects, or **table text** (see Creating text-based tables on p. 219) for row-and-column displays.

What's a text frame?

A text frame is effectively a mini-page, typically containing frame text in one or more paragraphs that flow through the frame. In WebPlus, frame text is called a **story**.

- When you select a frame you'll see its bounding box, indicated by a border line plus corner and edge handles, and (if you clicked with the Pointer Tool) a blinking insertion point in the frame's text. In this mode, you can edit the text with the Pointer Tool. (For details, see the topic Editing text on the page on p. 198.)

- When you move a text frame, its story text moves with it.

- When you resize a text frame, its story text reflows to the new dimensions.

Creating HTML frames

You add frames to a page as you would any other object. You can select, move, and resize any frame, but you cannot alter its basic shape. (See p. 227, 233, and 234, respectively.)

To create a frame:

1. Click the [HE] **HTML Text Frame Tool** button from the Text Frames flyout on the **Standard Objects** toolbar.

2. Click on the page or pasteboard to create a new frame at a default size.
   - or -
   Drag out to place the text frame at your chosen dimensions.

To delete a frame:

- Select the frame and press the **Delete** key. (If there's a selection point in the text, pressing **Delete** will remove characters after the cursor.)

Putting text into a frame

You can put text into a frame in one of several ways. The text will be converted to compliant HTML code.

WritePlus story editor: With a selected frame, click [A‡] **WritePlus** on the Frame context toolbar.

Importing text: Right-click on a frame and choose **Insert>Text File...** (shortcut **Ctrl+T**) to import text.

Typing into the frame:	Select the Pointer Tool, then click for an insertion point to type text straight into a frame, or edit existing text. (See Editing text on the page on p. 198.)
Pasting via the Clipboard:	At an insertion point in the text, press **Ctrl+V**.
Drag and drop:	Select text (e.g., in a word processor file), then drag it onto the WebPlus page. If you drop onto a selected frame, the text is pasted inline after existing text. Otherwise, a new frame is created for the text.

Frame setup and layout

The **frame layout** controls how text will flow in the frame. When a frame is selected and values for the margins are defined, its frame margins appear as dashed grey guide lines. These guides actually determine how text flows within the frame by providing padding between the text and frame edge. Text won't flow outside the frame margins.

Maecenas condimentum tincidunt lorem. Vestibulum vel tellus. Sed vulputate. Morbi massa nunc, convallis a, commodo gravida, tincidunt sed, turpis. Aenean ornare viverra est. Maecenas lorem. Aenean euismod iaculis dui. Sociis natoque penatibus et magnis dis parturient montes, nascetur ridiculus mus. Nulla quam. Aenean fermentum, turpis sed volutpat dignissim

To create frame margins:

- Select the frame, then drag column margin lines to adjust the boundaries of the column.

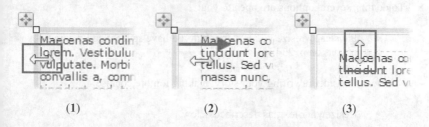

(1)   (2)   (3)

The illustration above shows how the cursor will change when hovering over the bounding box (**1**), after dragging inwards the frame margin can be adjusted (**2**), and after dragging downwards, the top frame margin can be moved (**3**).

> To allow frame margins to be set, ensure the frame is selected (and not frame text). The frame should show a solid bounding box.

For precise margin positioning, you can optionally create frame margins via dialog by defining the Left, Right, Top, or Bottom **Frame Margins**.

To create frame margins via dialog:

1. Select the HTML frame and click ![icon] **Frame Setup** on the Frame context toolbar.

2. From the dialog, you can define Frame Margins by setting **Left**, **Right**, **Top** and **Bottom** values.

Controlling overflowing frame text

Fitting story text precisely into text frames is part of the art of laying out websites. If there's too much story text to fit in your text frame, WebPlus stores it in an **overflow area** hidden from view (but not lost!) at the bottom of the frame.

![icon] The **Text overflow** button displays under the overflowing frame to indicate this hidden text, so it's important to ensure the text is made to display again, otherwise your story will remain truncated.

To do this, several options are open to you:

- Physically resize you text frame if you have space. See Resizing objects on p. 234.

- Consider rewriting your story, making it more concise!

- Resize your text, as described below.

To resize frame text once frames are sized and positioned, various tools are available on the Frame context toolbar.

 The **Text Sizing** flyout offers three tools for controlling how frame text scales through the text frame. These are "once-off" operations (compared to the "continuous" **Autofit** options shown below).

Fit Text
Click to scale the story's text size so it fits exactly into the available frame(s); further text added to the frame will cause text overflow. You can use this early on, to gauge how the story fits, or near the end, to apply the finishing touch. Fit Text first applies small point size changes, then small leading changes, then adjustments to the paragraph space below value, until the text fits.

Enlarge Text
Click to increase the story's text size one increment (approx. 2%).

Shrink Text
Click to reduce the story's text size one increment.

Each frame's story text can adopt its own individual autofit setting as follows:

 The **AutoFit Options** flyout offers three autofit options which continuously act upon a selected frame's story text.

No AutoFit
This is the normal mode of operation where, if selected, text won't automatically scale throughout the selected text frame.

Shrink Text on Overflow
If selected, extra text added to a selected frame will shrink all frame text to avoid text overflow.

AutoFit
If selected, the frame will always scale text automatically by adjusting text size (compare to **Fit Text** which fits text once, with any additional text causing text overflow).

For Creative frames, the Link button on the last frame of the sequence displays an **AutoFlow** and **Overflow** button. You might edit the story down or make more room for it by adding an extra frame or two to the sequence. Clicking the AutoFlow button adds additional frames and pages automatically as needed.

Using artistic text

Artistic text is standalone text you type directly onto a page. Especially useful for headlines, pull quotes, and other special-purpose text, it's easily formatted with the standard text tools.

Here are some similarities between frame text and artistic text. Both text types let you:

- vary character and paragraph properties, apply named text styles, edit text in WritePlus, and import text.

- apply different line styles, fills (including gradient and bitmap fills), and transparency.

- embed inline images.

- apply filter effects and rotate/flip.

- use proofing options such as AutoSpell/Spell Checker, Proof Reader, and Thesaurus.

- manage their content and track font usage via the Site Manager.

And some differences:

- You can initially "draw" artistic text at a desired point size, and drag it to adjust the size later. Frame text reflows in its frame upon frame resize.

- Artistic text can be applied to a path but frame text cannot.

- Artistic text won't automatically line wrap like frame text.

- Artistic text doesn't flow or link the way frame text does; the Frame context toolbar's text-fitting functions aren't applicable to artistic text.

To create artistic text:

1. Choose the **A** **Artistic Text Tool** from the **Standard Objects** toolbar's Text flyout.

2. Click anywhere on the page for an insertion point using a default point size, or drag to specify a particular size as shown here.

3. Set initial text properties (font, style, etc.) as needed before typing, using the Text context toolbar, **Text** menu, or right-click (choose **Text Format>**).

4. Type directly on the page to create the artistic text.

Once you've created an artistic text object, you can select, move, resize, delete, and copy it just as you would with a text frame. Solid colours, gradient/bitmap fills and transparency can all be applied.

To resize or reproportion an artistic text object:

- Drag the object's corner handles to resize it while maintaining the object's proportions.

- To resize freely, hold down the **Shift** key while dragging.

To edit artistic text:

- Drag to select a range of text, creating a blue selection.

You can also double-click to select a word.

Now you can type new text, apply character and paragraph formatting, edit the text in WritePlus, apply proofing options, and so on.

Putting text on a path

"Ordinary" straight-line artistic text is far from ordinary—but you can extend its creative possibilities even further by flowing it along a curved path.

The resulting object has all the properties of artistic text, plus its path is a Bézier curve that you can edit with the **Pointer Tool** as easily as any other line! In addition, text on a path is editable in some unique ways.

To apply a preset curved path to text:

1. Create an artistic text object.

2. With the text selected, click the  **Path flyout** on the Text context toolbar and choose a preset path.

The text now flows along the specified path, e.g., for "Path - Top Circle."

To add artistic text along an existing line or shape:

1. Create a freehand, straight, or curved line (see Drawing and editing lines on p. 297) or a shape (see Drawing and editing shapes on p. 303).

2. Choose the **A** **Artistic Text Tool** from the **Tools** toolbar's Text flyout.

3. Bring the cursor very close to the line. When the cursor changes to include a curve, click the mouse where you want the text to begin.

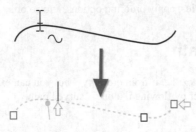

4. Begin typing at the insertion point. Text flows along the line, which has been converted to a path.

To fit existing text to an existing line or shape:

1. Create an artistic text object.

2. Create a freehand, straight, curved line or a shape.

3. Select both objects. On the **Tools** menu, choose **Fit Text to Curve**. The text now flows along the specified path.

To create text and path at the same time:

1. Choose one of the Path Text tools from the Text flyout:

    The **Freehand Path Text Tool** lets you sketch a curved line in a freeform way.

    The **Straight Path Text Tool** is for drawing a straight line.

    The **Curved Path Text Tool** lets you join a series of line segments (which may be curved or straight) using "connect the dots" mouse clicks.

2. Create a line on the page. Your line appears as a path with an insertion point at its starting end (for a curved path you can either type directly onto any part of the path or press **Esc** or double-click to get the insertion point at the start of the path).

3. Begin typing at the insertion point. Text flows along the path.

To remove the text path:

1. Select the path text object.

2. Click the ✕ **Path-None** button on the Text context toolbar's Path flyout.

The text remains as a straight-line artistic text object; the path is permanently removed.

Editing text on the page

You can use the Pointer Tool to edit frame text, table text, or artistic text directly. On the page, you can select and enter text, set paragraph indents and tab stops, change text properties, apply text styles, and use Find and Replace (see p. 200). For editing longer stories, and for more advanced options, choose WritePlus (**Edit Story...** from the **Edit** menu).

Selecting and entering text

The selection of frame text, artistic text, and table text follows the conventions of the most up-to-date word-processing tools. The selection area is shaded in semi-transparent blue for clear editing.

> Nulla vestibulum eleifend
> nulla. Suspendisse potenti.
> Aliquam turpis nisi, venenatis
> non, accumsan nec, imperdiet
> laoreet, lacus.

Double-, triple-, or quadruple-click selects a word, paragraph or all text, respectively. You can also make use of the **Ctrl**-click or drag for selection of non-adjacent words, and the **Shift** key for ranges of text.

To edit text on the page:

1. Select the **Pointer Tool**, then click (or drag) in the text object. A standard insertion point appears at the click position (see below).
    - or -
    Select a single word, paragraph or portion of text.

2. Type to insert new text or overwrite selected text, respectively.

> Nulla |vestibulum eleifend
> nulla. Suspendisse potenti.
> Aliquam turpis nisi, venenatis
> non, accumsan nec, imperdiet
> laoreet, lacus.

To start a new paragraph:

- Press **Enter**.

To start a new line within the same paragraph (using a "line break" or "soft return"):

- Press **Shift+Enter**.

To switch between insert mode and overwrite mode:

- Press the **Insert** key.

To repeat a text action:

- Choose **Repeat** from the **Edit** menu, or press **Ctrl+Y**.

For example, if you've applied new formatting to one paragraph, you can click in another paragraph and use **Repeat** to apply the same formatting there.

To show special characters:

- From the **View** menu, select **Special Characters** (for paragraph marks and breaks; see below) or **Spaces** (Show Special Characters, plus non-breaking spaces and "filled" normal spaces).

Copying, pasting and moving text

You can easily copy and paste text using standard commands; drag and drop of text is also supported. If you don't place an insertion point, the text can be pasted into a new text frame directly.

Setting paragraph indents

To set the indents of the current paragraph:

- Drag the appropriate ruler marker(s).
  - or –

- For quick left indents, select the **Increase Level** or
  Decrease Level button to increase or decrease indent, respectively.
  Indent is by the currently set default tab stop distance.
  - or -

- To adjust indent settings via a dialog, choose **Paragraph...** from the
  Text menu (or **Text Format>Paragraph...** from the right-click
  menu). In the Indentation box, you can enter values for Left, Right, 1st
  Line, or Hanging indents.

Working with Unicode text

WebPlus fully supports **Unicode**, making it possible to incorporate foreign
characters or special symbols.

- To paste Unicode text from the Clipboard to the page, use **Edit>Paste
  Special...,** then select "Unformatted Unicode Text."

- Insert Unicode characters directly into your text by typing your
  Unicode Hex value and pressing **Alt+X**. The Alt+X keyboard
  operation toggles between the displayed character (e.g., @) and its
  Hex value (e.g., U+0040) equivalent.

- To export text in Unicode format, use WritePlus.

Using Find and Replace

From **Edit> Find & Replace...** , you can search site text for an extraordinary
variety of items: not just words or parts of words, but a host of character and
paragraph attributes such as fonts, styles, alignment, bullets and numbering,
missing fonts, drop caps... even inline graphics and more! Using the Find and
Replace dialog—which remains open without interrupting your work until you
click its **Close** button—you can replace globally, or on a case-by-case basis.

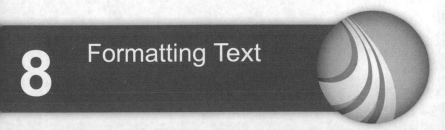

8 Formatting Text

Setting text properties

WebPlus gives you a high degree of control over the fine points of typographic layout, whether you're working with frame text, table text, or artistic text.

To apply basic text formatting:

1. Select the text.

2. Use buttons on the Text context toolbar to change text style, typeface, point size, attributes, paragraph alignment, or level.

To clear local formatting (restore plain/default text properties):

*   Select a range of text with local formatting.

*   Select **Ctrl**-Space Bar on your keyboard.

Using fonts

One of the most dramatic ways to change your site's appearance is to change the fonts used in your artistic text, frame text, or table text. Applying different fonts to a character or entire paragraph can communicate very different messages to your intended readership.

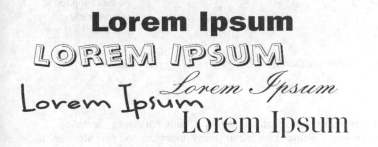

Font assignment is very simple in WebPlus, and can be done from the **Fonts** tab, Text context toolbar, or in the **Character** dialog (via right-click, or from the **Text** menu).

The Fonts tab lets you:

- Apply fonts easily without dialog navigation.

- Assign fonts to be Websafe or favourites.

- View most recently used, **Websafe**, and your favourite fonts simultaneously.

- Make a font rasterize on export or resolve its export in Site Checker.

- Search for installed fonts via search box.

- Hover-over preview of fonts applied to your site's text (optional).

Change a font for another throughout your site (by right-click Select All).

The Fonts tab is automatically hidden by default, but can be viewed by clicking the arrow button at the left of your workspace. You may also need to click the **Fonts** label to display the **Fonts** tab.

Websafe fonts are a specially selected and configurable subset of fonts which offer the best font matches between your site (during design) and your web visitors' computers (during browsing). On publishing, Websafe fonts are only referenced (and not rasterized) as they are assumed to be available on a web visitor's computer.

Generally speaking, it is advisable to keep to the standard list of Websafe fonts shown in the Fonts tab unless you can be sure of font usage amongst your target audience. These fonts are grouped together under the tab's Websafe category (an equivalent category exists on the text context toolbar's Font drop-down menu).

Using text styles

WebPlus lets you use named **text styles** (pre- or user-defined), which can be applied to frame text, table text, or artistic text. A text style is a set of character and/or paragraph attributes saved as a group. When you apply a style to text, you apply the whole group of attributes in just one step. For example, you could use named paragraph styles for particular layout elements, such as "Heading", "Quote", or "Body", and character styles to convey meaning, such as "Emphasis", "Code", or "Reference".

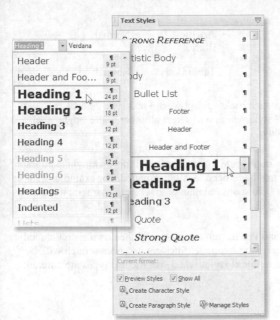

Styles can be applied to characters or paragraphs using either the Text context toolbar or the Text Styles tab. Both paragraph and character styles can be managed from the **Text Style Palette**.

The Text Styles tab also lets you create new styles from scratch, create named styles from existing text properties, and swap a style for another across your site in one operation. Any style can be previewed against any selected paragraph directly on the page. See online Help for more details on these features.

Paragraph styles and character styles

A **paragraph style** is a complete specification for the appearance of a paragraph, including all its font and paragraph format attributes. Every paragraph in WebPlus has a paragraph style associated with it.

- WebPlus includes a built-in **default** paragraph style called **"Normal"** which is left-aligned, 12pt Verdana. When you create different "body" text types, they'll have paragraph style names based on this "parent" text style.

Text Type	Paragraph Style used	Based on
Frame (HTML or Creative)	Body	Normal
Artistic	Artistic Body	Normal
Table/Calendar	Table Body	Normal

This hierarchical approach makes for powerful text style control. You can modify the "Normal" style which will affect all other "child" styles such as Body and Artistic Body.

- Applying a paragraph style to text updates all the text in the paragraph except sections that have been locally formatted. For example, a single word marked as bold would remain bold when the paragraph style was updated or changed.

- Theme layouts and Pro design templates use their own preset named styles depending on the template. Sites created from scratch will, by default, use different text styles when specific text types are entered.

A **character style** includes only font attributes (name, point size, bold, italic, etc.), and you apply it at the character level—that is, to a range of selected characters—rather than to the whole paragraph.

- Typically, a character style applies emphasis (such as italics, bolding or colour) to whatever underlying font the text already uses; the assumption is that you want to keep that underlying font the same. The base character style is shown in the Text Styles tab (or palette) as **"Default Paragraph Font,"** which has no specified attributes but basically means "whatever font the paragraph style already uses."

- Applying the Default Paragraph Font option from the Text Styles tab (or the Text context toolbar's Styles box) will strip any selected local character formatting you've added and will restore original text attributes (paragraph styles are not affected).

- As with paragraph styles, you can define any number of new character styles using different names and attributes (or adopt a pre-defined character style).

Working with named styles

Body ▾   The named style of the currently selected text is displayed in either the Text Styles tab or the drop-down **Styles** box on the Text context toolbar. A character style (if one is applied locally) may be shown; otherwise it indicates the paragraph style.

To apply a named style:

1. Using the Pointer Tool, click in a paragraph (if applying a paragraph style) or select a range of text (if applying a character style). If you apply a paragraph style, it will be applied to the whole paragraph regardless of the amount of text selected. If you've selected text in more than one paragraph, the change takes place in all selected paragraphs.

2. Display the **Text Styles** tab and select a style from the style list.
   - or -
   On the Text context toolbar, click the arrow to expand the Styles drop-down list and select a style name.

The Text Style tab highlights the paragraph or character style applied to any selected text.

As both paragraph and character formatting can be applied to the same text, all of the current text's formatting is displayed in the **Current format** box on the tab. In the example below, currently selected text has a Strong character style applied over a Normal paragraph style.

> **Current format:** Body + Strong

To modify an existing style:

1. From the Text Styles tab:

   - Right-click on the character or paragraph style you want to modify and then choose **Modify <style>....**
     - or -

   - With a style selected, pick the Manage Styles button from the **Text Styles** tab, then choose the **Modify...** button.

2. From the Text Style dialog, define (or change) the style name, base style, and any character or paragraph attributes, tabs, bullets, and drop caps you want to include in the style definition.

3. Click **OK** to accept style properties, or **Cancel** to abandon changes.

4. Click **Apply** to update text, or click **Close** to maintain the style in the site for future use.

Alternatively, choose **Text Style Palette...** from the **Text** menu to modify styles and to change text defaults (see p. 241).

To delete one or more text styles:

- Right-click a text style and select **Delete <style>....**

- From the dialog, click **Remove**. For deletion of multiple styles, check multiple style names first. For removal of all or unused styles, use appropriate buttons.

⚠ Take care when deleting styles. Styles based on a checked "parent" style will be checked for deletion.

Changing common styles

Changing one character or paragraph style for another is very simple for a single portion of text. However, in WebPlus, it's just as easy to swap one style for another by selecting multiple instances of the style and choosing an alternative style. This swaps styles across paragraphs and throughout entire stories all at the same time.

To select (and change) a style throughout your site:

1. Right-click a style displayed on the **Text Styles** tab.

2. If the style is used in your site, you'll see a "*Select All **n** instance(s)*" message (***n*** is the number of times the style is used).

   If there are no occurrences of the style, the option is greyed out.

3. Click the message label—text formatted with the chosen style is highlighted.

4. Hover over style names in your styles list. Click on a chosen style to apply the style to the selected text.

Creating a bulleted or numbered list

For any text frame it's possible to apply bullets and numbering to lists and paragraphs alike. Bullets are especially useful when listing items of interest in no specific order of preference and numbered lists for presenting step-by-step procedures (by number or letter). WebPlus lets you apply the list style to normal text (as local formatting) or to text styles equally.

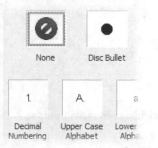

None   Disc Bullet

1.   A.   a

Decimal   Upper Case   Lower
Numbering   Alphabet   Alpha

Within HTML text frames, basic bullet icons, numbers (numeric and Roman) and letters can be applied.

However, if you're using Creative text frames you can adopt basic as well as complex **bulleted** or **numbered** lists either by selecting presets (see below) or creating your own custom list style (these let you select your own symbols, numbers and letter formats). You then have the option of replacing an existing preset with your own preset based on your custom list style.

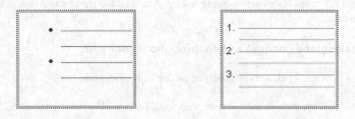

| Bulleted list | Numbered list |

To create a simple bulleted or numbered list:

1. Select one or more paragraphs.
   - or -
   Click in a paragraph's text.

2. Select ⦂≡ **Bulleted List** or ≡ **Numbered List** from the Text context toolbar.

The list style used is the first preset shown in the Bullets & Numbering dialog described below.

To create a bulleted or numbered list (using presets):

1. Select one or more paragraphs.
   - or -
   Click in a paragraph's text.

2. Select **Bullets and Numbering...** from the **Text** menu.

3. From the Text Style dialog, either:

   - For text in HTML text frames, click in a preset icon from the dialog (see above).
     - or -

- For text in Creative text frames, pick **Bullet** or **Number** from the **Style** drop-down menu, then select one of the preset formats shown by default.
  - or -

- For a custom list, select a preset then click the **Details** button to alter custom options.

4. Click **OK** to apply list formatting.

Each time you insert a following return, a new line will begin with the specified symbol or number. In addition, typing two returns in a row (pressing **Enter** twice) cancels bullets or numbers and resumes regular paragraph formatting.

Turn off list formatting by clicking the Text context toolbar's ⋮≡ or ⅟₂≡ buttons again.

To restart list numbering (Creative frame text only):

1. Click to place an insertion point in the list to set the restart position, then select **Bullets & Numbering...** from the **Text** menu.

2. From the Presets or Details page, check **Restart Numbering** to reset the number or letter sequence back to 1 or A, respectively.

3. Click **OK**.

To turn off bullets or numbering formatting:

1. Select the paragraph with list formatting.

2. Select **Text>Bullets and Numbering...** from the **Text** menu.
   - or -
   Right-click the paragraph and from the **Text Format** option, choose **Bullets and Numbering...**.

3. In the **Text Styles** dialog, click the **None** preset option.

WebPlus also lets you assign bullets and numbers to styles. (See WebPlus help.)

Inserting user details

You can take advantage of the **User Details** dialog to store frequently-used or updated user information so you don't need to keep re-entering it—think of how often a mobile phone number or email address may change over time! The dialog lets you review all your User Details at a glance, and will update fields throughout your website directly.

For managing user details across multiple business sites, WebPlus supports different business sets (i.e., a stored set of user details) which can be applied per website.

These fields need to be present on your site pages in advance of updates and may have to be inserted manually via **Insert>Information>User Details**. Note that many design templates already have these user detail fields present, e.g. on contact pages.

You can also use this User Details dialog to define global and site-specific **variables** for use in all WebPlus sites or just the current site, respectively. (See Inserting variables on p. 215.)

To add, edit or change User Details:

1. Click **Set User Details** on the Default context toolbar.

2. For business user details, enter new information in the **Business Sets** tab. Ensure the **Select Set** drop-down list is set to Default if you're only likely to use one set of business details. The drop-down list lets you select a different set of business user details, if created. (See Creating business sets on p. 214).

3. For home users details, use the **Home** tab. These fields are distinct from those set in the Business Sets tab.

> A **Calendars** tab will appear if there is a calendar in your site. This lets you change the year and show/hide public holidays and personal events.

Inserting and updating user details

You can insert one or more User Details fields into your site at any time.

To insert a User Detail field:

1. Select the Pointer Tool and click in the text for an insertion point.

2. Choose **Information** from the **Insert** menu, then **User Details...**.

3. Select a User Detail entry, and optionally any text **Prefix** or suffix (**Postfix**) to include with your user details, e.g. *Name:*.

4. Click **OK**.

For existing sites, the fields (once edited) can be updated at the click of a button.

To update fields:

- Enter new information in the User Details dialog (via **Tools>Set User Details...**).

- Click the **Update** button to automatically update any altered field currently placed in your site. This field will remain linked to User Details until it is deleted.

Creating business sets

If you are developing more than one business site, you can store and assign different sets of business user details for each site. Think of a business set as a profile, storing a unique set of user details under a chosen name.

To create a business set:

1. From the User Details dialog (Business Sets tab), click **New...**.

2. Enter a new name for the business set and click **OK**. Your new set becomes active as shown in the **Select Set** drop-down list.

3. Enter information in the User Details dialog, then click **Update**.

Once you've created a business set and applied it to your site, the settings will be stored with the site.

Business sets allow you to store different user details for each website you create.

To swap to a different business set:

- Select an alternative set from the **Select Set** drop-down list, then click **Update**.

To rename or delete a business set:

1. Choose the business set from the **Select Set** drop-down list.

2. Select **Rename** or **Delete**.

Inserting variables

If you have some repeating text used throughout your site which you'd like to swap for replacement text, you can use **variables**. Typically, you would do this to change a product name or version, making your site easy to update when product names or versions change. The variable fields change automatically, updating with the new values.

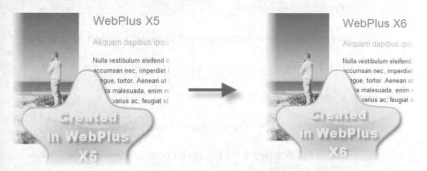

Variables are used in a similar way to user details (see p. 212). They can be added and inserted just like user detail fields and be updated from the same User Details dialog.

The variable can be stored just within the site or made global for other sites. The latter would be a good choice for product names as they are likely to be used again globally in a company environment.

To add, edit or delete variables:

1. Click **Set User Details** on the default context toolbar (deselect objects to view).

2. Select the **Global** or **Site** tab if you want the added variable to be available to all sites or just to the site, respectively.

3.   From either tab, click the **Add** button.

4.   In the variables list, type over the created **Variable** name, giving it a
     unique string that identifies the variable easily.

Variable	Value
Product_Name_Version	

5.   Click in the column adjacent to the new Variable and type the variable
     value (i.e. the text that will appear on the page).

Variable	Value
Product_Name_Version	WebPlus X5

6.   Add additional variables as required to either the Site or Global tab.

7.   Click **Update**.

To insert a variable field:

1.   Click in the text for an insertion point (or make a text selection).

2.   Choose **Information** from the **Insert** menu, then select **Variable...**
     from the submenu.

3.   From the dialog's drop-down list, select your variable from where you
     stored it in User Details (Global or Site).

4.   Select a variable entry, and optionally any text **Prefix** or **Suffix** to
     include with your variable.

5.   Click **OK**.

When you want to change the variable, all that's needed is to edit and update the
variable's value.

To update variables:

1.   From the User Details dialog, edit the existing variable with a new
     value.

2.   Click **Update**.

9 Working
with Tables

Creating text-based tables

Tables are ideal for presenting text and data in a variety of easily customizable row-and-column formats, with built-in spreadsheet capabilities.

			£/€
Ranunculus aquatilis	345-56	1	4.24/4.97
Myosotis scorpiodes	334-B299	2	4.64/5.44
Nymphoides peltata	089-78	2	2.93/3.44
Menyanthes trifoliate	455-01	1	7.10/8.32
Caltha palustris	345-33	1	2.55/2.99

Each cell in a table behaves like a mini-frame. Like frame text you can vary character and paragraph properties, apply named text styles, embed inline images, apply solid text colour fills, and use proofing options such as Spell Checker, Proof Reader, and Thesaurus. Some unique features include number formatting and formula insertion.

Two types of table can be applied to the WebPlus page—the HTML table and the Creative table. The most commonly used table type used in WebPlus is **HTML table**, as they are HTML compatible, ensuring good published results across all Internet browsers.

However, **Creative tables** can be used instead of HTML tables for additional table features such as table rotation, gradient/bitmap fills, text transparency, filter effects, Instant3D, and Warp effects.

Creating tables

Rather than starting from scratch, WebPlus is supplied with a selection of pre-defined table formats, i.e. templates, that can be used. Simply pick one and fill in the cells with content.

WebPlus lets you:

- Edit the pre-defined format before adding a new table to the page.

- Create your own custom formats without creating a table. See Creating custom table formats in online Help.

- Edit existing tables to fit a different format (pre-defined or custom).

To create a table:

1. On the **Standard Objects** toolbar (▾ Table flyout), choose **HTML Table Tool**.

2. Click on the page or pasteboard, or drag to set the table's dimensions. The Create Table dialog appears with a selection of preset table formats shown in the **Format** window.

3. Step through the list to preview the layouts and select one (use up/down keyboard arrows for a "live" preview of each). To begin with a plain table, select **(Default)**.

4. (Optional) Click **Edit** if you want to further customize your chosen format.

5. Set the **Table Size**. This is the number of rows and columns that make up the table layout.

6. Click **OK**. The new table appears on the page.

To modify the structure and cell contents of tables, please see Manipulating tables in online Help.

Inserting a calendar

The **Calendar Wizard** helps you design month-at-a-glance calendars for use on your web page.

JANUARY 2011	
1	S
2	S
3	M
4	T
5	W
6	T
7	F

The calendar is created as a scalable text-based table so you can edit text using the standard text tools. The properties of a selected calendar are similar to those of a table, and can be modified identically (see Manipulating tables). Like custom table formats you can create your own custom calendar formats.

The wizard lets you set up the month/year and calendar style/format, and controls the inclusion of personal events and/or public holidays. The **Calendar Event Manager** lets you add personal events before or after adding a calendar to the page.

For calendar-specific properties, a context toolbar lets you change an existing calendar's month/year, modify calendar-specific properties, and manage calendar events (both personal and public holidays).

At any time, you can update calendar details throughout your site via **Set User Details**—in the same way that you'd set up the date (along with the time) on some alarm clocks. This is especially useful if you want to update the year on a year-to-view web page, composed of 12 monthly calendars—you only need to change the year in one place.

To insert a calendar:

1. 〈〉 ▾ 31 Click the **Table** flyout on the **Standard Objects** toolbar and choose **Insert Calendar**.

2. Click again on your page, or drag out to indicate the desired size of the calendar.

3. From the displayed **Calendar Wizard**, define options for your calendar including setting the year and month, calendar style (square, or in single or multiple column format), week start day, display options, switching on personal events/holidays, and calendar format.

    To have your country's public holidays shown, check **Add public holidays** in the wizard and select a **Region** from the associated drop-down menu. To add personal events, check **Add personal events** additionally.

4. Click **Finish** to complete the wizard.

> ✎ If you plan to use your calendar in subsequent years, simply update the **Year** setting in **Tools>Set User Details**.

To view and edit a selected calendar's properties:

1. Click the **Edit Calendar** button on the Calendar context toolbar.

2. Choose an appropriate tab (Date, Style, Events, etc.) and make your modification, then press **OK**.

Right-click (with the **Calendar** option selected) also lets you select, insert, distribute, delete, and adjust widths/heights for rows (or columns), as well as autofit to cell contents, but take care not to corrupt your table formatting!

Adding public holidays

When you create a calendar you can set up the appropriate public holidays for the country you reside in. The holidays will show up in your calendar automatically if **Add public holidays** is checked in Calendar Properties.

To enable public holidays:

1. Select your calendar's bounding box, and click 📅 **Edit Calendar** on the context toolbar.

2. From the Events tab, check **Add public holidays**.

3. (Optional) Swap to a different country's public holiday settings by using the **Region** drop-down list.

4. Click **OK**.

To display public holidays:

1. Select your calendar's bounding box.

2. Click **Calendar Events** on the context toolbar.

3. Enable the **Show public holidays** option.

Adding personal events

JANUARY 2011		
1	S	
2	S	
3	M	Holiday Leave
4	T	Wedding Anniversary
5	W	
6	T	
7	F	Laura's Birthday

You can complement your public holiday listings (e.g., Easter holidays) by adding personal events such as birthdays, anniversaries, and bill payments (unfortunately!) so that the events show up on your calendar—simply use the **Calendar Events** button on a selected calendar's context toolbar. Events show automatically on your calendar under the chosen date.

To add an event:

1. Select your calendar's bounding box.

2. Click 🗓 **Calendar Events** on the context toolbar.

3. (Optional) Check **Show events by date** to add, edit, or delete events using a traditional calendar layout. Leave unchecked for a row-by-row Date/Event listing.

4. Click 📝 **New event**.

5. From the dialog, type, use the up/down arrows, or click the ⬜ **Browse** button to select a date.

6. Enter your event text into the text input box, This displays in your calendar under the chosen date.

7. If the event is a birthday or other annual event, check **Event recurs annually**.

8. Click **OK**. The event appears in the event list under the chosen date.

9. When you have finished adding events, click the **Save** button.

🖝 Use the 📋 **Edit Event** or ✕ **Delete Event** buttons to modify or delete an existing event.

10 Editing Objects

Selecting an object

 Before you can change any object, you need to select it using one of the following tools from the **Tools** toolbar's Selection flyout:

 Pointer Tool
Click to use the **Pointer Tool** to select, move, copy, resize or rotate objects.

Lasso Tool
Click to use the **Lasso Tool** to draw a freeform region under which any objects will become selected.

 Rotate Tool
Click to use the **Rotate Tool** to rotate an object around a rotation origin (normally centred). See Rotating an object on p. 235.

Prior to any selection, WebPlus objects will display a "glowing" selection hover highlight around the object. In a complex grouping of objects, this indicates which object will become selected.

To select an object:

- Click on the object using one of the tools shown above, to reveal a bounding box around the object.

💡 If items overlap, use the **Alt** key while clicking repeatedly until the desired item is selected.

To select an object with the Lasso Tool:

1. Select the 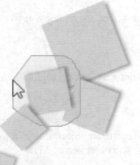 **Lasso Tool**.

2. Draw a "lasso" around the object(s) you want to select. A shaded lasso region is created around the object.

3. Release the mouse button. All of the objects within the lasso region are selected.

💡 If attempting to lasso an object within a group, remember to ungroup the objects first.

💡 To avoid picking up an object under your cursor, keep the **Shift** key pressed as you draw the lasso.

🖈 If you prefer to keep the Pointer Tool selected, you can lasso objects as described above with the **Alt** key pressed.

When selecting a text object with the Pointer Tool:

- Clicking on a text object (artistic text or text frame) with the Pointer Tool selects the object and also positions the blinking text selection cursor within the object's text. In this mode, you can edit the text (see p. 198).

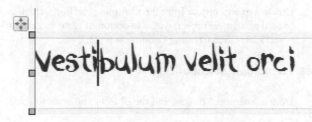

- Double-, triple-, or quadruple-click to select a word, paragraph, or all text.

- To select only the text frame, click the frame's bounding box.

- Clicking on a group selects the grouped object. **Ctrl**-click to select an individual object within a group.

Selecting objects via Objects tab

To select an object:

1. From the **Objects tab**, select the page on which your objects are placed.

2. Expand the page entry by clicking ⊞ **Expand**, revealing objects on the page.

3. Select your object.

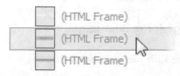

You can use **Ctrl**-click and **Shift**-click to select multiple non-adjacent or adjacent object entries.

Selecting multiple objects

Selecting more than one object at a time (creating a **multiple selection**) lets you:

- Position or resize all the objects at the same time.

- Create a **group object** from the multiple selection, which can then be treated as a single object, with the option of restoring the individual objects later. See Creating Groups on p. 250.

To create a multiple selection:

- Drag a "marquee" box around the objects you want to select.

Alternatively, hold down the **Shift** key and click each object in turn, or use the Lasso Tool (p. 227) to draw around objects to select them.

> The last selected object is shown with a darker bounding box when compared to other selected objects.

To add or remove objects from a multiple selection:

- Hold down the **Shift** key and click the object to be added or removed.

To deselect all objects in a multiple selection:

- Click in a blank area of the workspace.

To select all objects on the page (or master page):

- Choose **Select All** from the **Edit** menu (or press **Ctrl+A**).

Copying, pasting, and replicating objects

Besides using the Windows Clipboard to copy and paste objects, you can duplicate objects easily using drag-and-drop, and replicate multiple copies of any object in precise formations. You can also transfer the formatting of one object to another, with the option of selecting specific attributes to be included when formatting is pasted.

To copy an object (or multiple selection) to the Windows Clipboard:

- Click 🖺 **Copy** on the **Standard** toolbar.

If you're using another Windows application, you can usually copy and paste objects via the Clipboard.

To paste an object from the Clipboard:

- Click 🖺 **Paste** on the **Standard** toolbar.

The standard Paste command inserts the object at the insertion point or (for a separate object) at the centre of the page. To insert a separate object at the same page location as the copied item, use the **Paste in Place** command.

To choose between alternative Clipboard formats:

- Choose **Paste Special...** from the **Edit** menu.

To duplicate an object:

1. Select the object, then press the **Ctrl** key.

2. Drag the object via the 🕂 **Move** button to a new location on the page, then release the mouse button.

3. To constrain the position of the copy (to same horizontal or vertical), press and hold down the **Shift** key while dragging. A duplicate of the object appears at the new location.

Replicating objects

Duplicating an object means making just one copy at a time. The **Replicate** command lets you create multiple copies in a single step, with precise control over how the copies are arranged, either as a linear series or a grid. You can include one or more transformations to produce an interesting array of rotated and/or resized objects. It's great for repeating backgrounds, or for perfectly-aligned montages of an image or object.

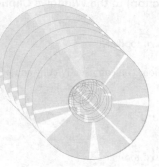

To replicate an object:

1. Select the object to be replicated and choose **Replicate...** from the **Edit** menu. The Replicate dialog appears, with a preview region at the right.

2. To arrange copies in a straight line, select **Create line**. For an X-by-Y grid arrangement, select **Create grid**.

3. Specify **Line length** (the number of objects including the original) in the arrangement, or the Grid size. Note that you can use the Line length setting to include an odd number of objects in a grid.

4. Set spacing between the objects as either an **Offset** (measured between the top left corners of successive objects) or a **Gap** (between the bottom right and top left corners). You can specify **Horizontal** and/or **Vertical** spacing, and/or an angular **Rotation**. To set a specific horizontal or vertical interval, check **Absolute**; uncheck the box to specify the interval as a percentage of the original object's dimensions.

5. Click **OK**.

The result is a multiple selection. Click its ⊞ **Group** button if you want to keep the separate objects linked for additional manipulations.

Pasting an object's formatting

Once you have copied an object to the Clipboard, you can use **Paste Format** (**Edit** menu) to apply its formatting attributes to another **selected** object. Again from the **Edit** menu, **Paste Format Plus** displays a "master control" dialog that lets you select or deselect specific attributes to be included when formatting is pasted. See Saving object styles on p. 314 for more dialog information.

Moving objects

To move an object (including a multiple selection):

- Drag the selected object by using its ⊕ **Move** button. Once you see a move cursor you can begin dragging.

💡 To set exact horizontal and vertical positions, use the **Transform tab**.

To constrain the movement of an object to horizontal or vertical:

- Select the object and use the keyboard arrows (up, down, left, right).

Resizing objects

WebPlus provides several methods of resizing lines, shapes, artistic text, text frames, and tables. Click-and-drag is the simplest—watch the Hintline for context-sensitive tips and shortcuts!

To resize an object (in general):

1. Select the object.

2. Click one of the object's handles and drag it to a new position while holding down the left mouse button.

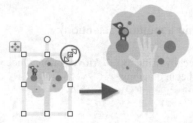

Dragging from an edge handle resizes in one dimension, by moving that edge. Dragging from a corner handle resizes in two dimensions, by moving two edges.

> ✎ You can also make fine resizing adjustments from the **Transform tab**.

To resize freely:

*   Drag from a corner (or line end) handle.

To constrain a shape, frame object, or table object when resizing:

*   Hold the **Shift** key down and drag from a corner (or line end) handle.

For shapes, this has the effect of keeping a square as a square, a circle as a circle, etc.

> ✎ For pictures, dimensions are constrained on dragging a corner handle. Use **Shift**-drag to resize a picture freely.

Rotating an object

You can rotate single and multiple objects, including pictures, text objects, and groups using the object's rotation handle or the Rotate Tool.

To rotate a selected object (using its rotation handle):

- Click and drag the rotation handle extending from the selection box (use the **Shift** key while dragging for 15° rotation intervals).

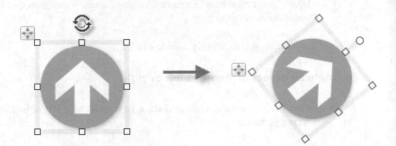

To rotate an object (using Rotate Tool):

1. From the **Tools** toolbar's ![Selection flyout] Selection flyout, select the ![Rotate Tool] **Rotate Tool**.

2. Click to select the object, hover over one of its edge or corner handles until you see the rotate cursor.

3. Hold the mouse button down and drag the cursor in the direction in which you want to rotate the object, then release (use the **Shift** key for 15° rotation intervals).

The Pointer Tool can also be used to rotate objects in the same way (with the ↶ cursor).

To undo rotation (then restore the original orientation):

- Double-click the object.

- To restore the rotated position, double-click again.

To change the rotation origin:

1. Select the  **Rotate Tool** and click to select the object.

2. Move the rotation origin ⊕ away from its original position in the centre of the object to any position on the page. The origin can also be moved to be outside the object—ideal for rotating grouped objects around a central point.

3. Drag the rotation handle to a new rotation angle—the object will rotate about the new origin.

To reset the rotation origin, simply double-click it.

To rotate an object 90 degrees left or right:

- Select the object and choose **Rotate Left** or **Rotate Right** from the **Arrange** menu.

Cropping and combining objects

Cropping means masking (hiding) parts of an object, for example to improve composition or to create a special effect. The underlying object is intact. Two types of cropping are possible—**square** cropping or **irregular** cropping.

square crop   *irregular crop*

Combining starts with more than one object, but creates a special composite object with one or more "holes" on the inside where the component objects' fills overlapped one another—useful for creating mask or stencil effects.

To crop using the object's original outline:

1. Select the object, then select the ⊏⊐ **Square Crop Tool** from the **Tools** toolbar's Effects flyout.

2. Drag one of its edge or corner handles inward for unconstrained cropping. Press the **Shift** key while dragging for constrained cropping (aspect ratio is maintained).

To scale the object within the crop outline, **Ctrl**-drag either upwards or downwards.

To crop by modifying the object's outline:

*   Select the object, then select the ⊠ **Irregular Crop Tool** from the **Tools** toolbar's Effects flyout. The Curve context toolbar appears, which lets you control the displayed nodes and connecting segments that define the object's crop outline.

    *   To move a node (control point) where you see the ⁻₁⁻ cursor, drag the node.

    *   To move a line segment (between two nodes) where you see the cursor, drag the segment.

To position a cropped object within its crop outline:

*   With either crop tool selected, click the object and drag its centre (when you see the hand cursor).

To feather the crop outline:

*   With either crop tool selected, click the object.

*   From the Crop context toolbar, set a **Feather** value using the up/down arrows, slider or by direct input. Feathering is applied outside the crop outline by the set point size.

To uncrop (restore full visibility):

- Click the **Remove Crop** button on the Crop context toolbar.

Cropping to a shape

The **Crop to Shape** command works with exactly two objects selected. Either or both of these may be a group object. The lower object (the one behind the other) gets clipped to the outline of the upper object, leaving a shape equivalent to the overlapping region.

To crop to shape:

1. Place the "clipping" object in front of the object to be cropped, using the **Arrange** menu and/or **Arrange** toolbar as needed. In the illustration above, a QuickShape (Quick Thought Bubble) is in front of a holiday.

2. With both objects selected (or grouped), choose **Crop to Shape** from the **Tools** menu.

Combining lines and shapes

Combining curves is a way of creating a composite object from two or more lines or drawn shapes. As with cropping to a shape, the object in front clips the object(s) behind, in this case leaving one or more "holes" where the component objects overlapped. As with grouping, you can apply formatting (such as line or fill) to the combined object and continue to edit individual nodes and segments with the Pointer Tool. Unlike those other methods, a combined object permanently takes the line and fill properties of the front object. Combining is reversible, but the component objects keep the line and fill properties of the combined object.

Combining is a quick way to create a mask or stencil cutout:

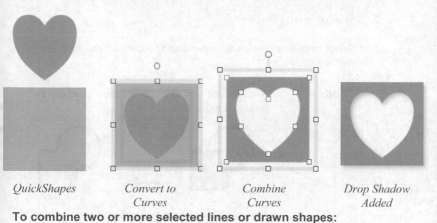

QuickShapes   *Convert to*   *Combine*   *Drop Shadow*
                   Curves   *Curves*   *Added*

To combine two or more selected lines or drawn shapes:

1. Draw your two lines or QuickShapes.

2. Place the "clipping" object in front of the object to be cut out, using the **Arrange** menu and/or **Arrange** toolbar as needed.

3. Select each object and choose **Tools>Convert to Curves**.

4. Select both objects.

5. Choose **Combine Curves** from the **Arrange** menu.

To restore the original shapes from a combined object:

- Select the combined object and choose **Split Curves** from the **Arrange** menu.

Joining object outlines

WebPlus includes some powerful tools to carve new shapes out of old overlapping shapes. With add, subtract, intersect, or exclude commands you actually produce a permanent new object (with a new outline) out of any selected objects. The joined object can be further edited by adjusting nodes in the new shape.

To join outlines:

7.   Select objects.

8.   Select an outlines option from the **Join Outlines** submenu on the **Arrange** menu.

   Add   Creates one new object that's the sum of any two
                      selected objects.

                      The objects need not be overlapping.

   Subtract   Discards the overlap between the top and bottom
                      object. The bottom object is also discarded.

                      Useful as a quick way of truncating shapes and
                      pictures with another object.

                      Ensure the objects are overlapping!

   Intersect   Retains the overlap and discards the rest.

Exclude   Merges two or more objects into a composite object, with a clear transparent "hole" where their filled regions overlap.

Updating and saving defaults

Object defaults are the stored property settings WebPlus applies to newly created objects such as:

- **lines** and **shapes** (line and fill colour, shade, pattern, transparency, etc.)

- **frames** (margins, columns, etc.)

- **text** (i.e., font, size, colour, alignment, etc.). Defaults are saved separately for **artistic, shape**, **frame** and **table text.**

You can easily change the defaults for any type of object via the **Update Object Default** command or the **Text Style Palette** dialog.

Default settings are always **local**—that is, any changed defaults apply to the current site and are automatically saved with it, so they're in effect next time you open that site. However, at any time you can use the **Save Defaults** command to record the current defaults as **global** settings that will be in effect for any new site you subsequently create.

To set local defaults for a particular type of object:

1. Create a single sample object and fine-tune its properties as desired— or use an existing object that already has the right properties. (For graphics, you can use a line, shape, or rectangle; all share the same set of defaults.)

2. Select the object that's the basis for the new defaults and choose **Update Object Default** from the **Format** menu.

Or, for line and fill colours, including line styles:

1. With no object selected, choose the required line and/or fill colours from the Colour or Swatches tab (see Applying solid colours on p. 319). Use the Line tab to set a default line weight, style, and corner shape.

2. Draw your object on the page, which will automatically adopt the newly defined default colours and styles.

To view and change default text properties:

1. Choose **Text Style Palette...** from the **Text** menu.

2. Click **Default Text**, then from the expanded list of text types, choose an option (e.g., Artistic Text).

3. Click **Modify...** to view current settings for the selected text type.

4. Use the Text Style dialog to alter character, paragraph, and bullet/list properties.

To save all current defaults as global settings:

1. Select **Save Defaults...** from the **Tools** menu.

2. From the dialog, check options to update specific defaults globally:

    - **Document and object defaults** - saves current site settings (page size, orientation) and object settings (context toolbar settings).

    - **Text styles** - saves current text styles in the Text Style Palette.

    - **Object styles** - saves user-defined styles from Styles tab.

    - **Table and calendar formats** - saves custom formats saved in Table Formats dialog.

3. Click **Save** to confirm that you want new sites to use the checked object's defaults globally.

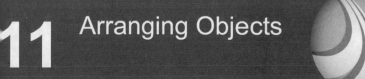

11 Arranging Objects

Ordering objects

As objects are created, they are **stacked** in the order you create them, from back to front, with each new object in front of the others. At any time, you can change the stacking order, which affects how objects appear on the page.

To shift the object's position one step toward the front or back:

- Click 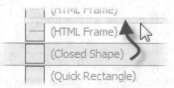 **Forward One** or **Back One** on the **Arrange** toolbar, respectively.

To shift the selected object's position to the bottom or top of the stack:

- Click **Send to Back** or **Bring to Front** on the **Arrange** toolbar, respectively.

If you're working with complex arrangements of objects, perhaps needing more control when reordering, you can use the Objects tab.

To shift object positions via Objects tab:

1. From the Objects tab, select the page on which you objects are placed.

2. Expand the page entry by clicking ⊞ **Expand**, revealing objects on the page.

3. Select and drag your object to a new position in the object list.

You can use **Ctrl**-click and **Shift**-click to select multiple non-adjacent or adjacent object entries.

💡 The highest object in the list is the highest in the object order.

Aligning and distributing objects

Alignment involves taking a group of selected objects and aligning them all in one operation by their top, bottom, left or right edges. You can also distribute objects, so that your objects (as a multiple selection) are spread evenly (optionally at spaced intervals).

Alignment or distribution can occur between the endmost objects on your page (current selection), page margins, or the page edge.

Alignment to last selected object lets you choose a specific object in a multiple selection from which to align other objects.

As other alignment methods, use layout guides, dynamic guides, or a dot grid combined with snapping to assist you in placing objects on the page. See WebPlus help for more information.

To align the edges of two or more objects in a selection:

1. Using the Pointer Tool, **Shift**-click on all the objects you want to align, or draw a marquee box around them, to create a multiple selection.

2. Select the Align tab.

3. Select an option for vertical and/or horizontal alignment. Choose **Top**, **Bottom**, **Left**, **Right**, **Centre Horizontally** or **Centre Vertically**.

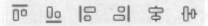

To distribute two or more objects across a selection:

- Choose   **Space Evenly Across** or   **Space Evenly Down** to spread selected objects uniformly between endmost objects in the current selection (horizontally or vertically, respectively) or by a set measurement (choose **Spaced** and set a value in any measurement unit).

Rather than work within the current selection area you can align or distribute to page margins (if set) or page edge.

To align/distribute objects to page margins or edges:

Relative to: Selection ▼

Selection
Last Selected
Margins
Page

- Select from the **Relative to** drop-down menu to align the selected object(s) within the page **Margins** or **Page** edges then choose an align or distribute button described above.

For more advanced alignment control, you can align multiple objects in relation to your last selected object (select objects in turn with the **Shift** key pressed) by using the **Relative to: Last Selected** drop-down list option.

> The last selected object is shown with a darker bounding box when compared to other selected objects.

Attaching objects to text

WebPlus lets you position shapes, pictures, or gallery objects in relation to your site's text (artistic or frame text) in one of two ways:

- **Float with text**. This option is ideal for pictures and shapes, etc.

Miles Militis

Suspendisse sem lorem, ornare n
vestibulum ut, tempor porttitor, est
convallis aliquet eros. Nunc nec n
urna convallis eleifend. Nulla feug
augue. Integer feugiat nisi vitae ve

*A shape attached
to artistic text such as titles*

Epulae Epulae -
15/09/2009

Suspendisse sem
lorem, ornare non,
vestibulum ut, tempor
porttitor, est. Quisque convallis aliquet eros
Nunc nec nulla eget urna convallis eleifend
Nulla feugiat eros at augue. Integer feugiat

*A picture within
a text frame*

- **Position inline as character**. The attached object is placed as a character in the text and vertically aligned in relation to the text that surrounds it.

A gallery object attached to an artistic text title

A "Fun" gallery object positioned inline within a text frame

The advantage of both methods, is that the object associated with the text will move as your text is moved. For frame text especially, when the text reflows as new content is added to the frame, the attached object will move with the text.

To attach an object to text:

1. Position the object over or close to the artistic text or text frame to be attached to.

2. Select **Attach to Text...** from the **Arrange** menu.

3. From the dialog, choose a positioning option:

Either, for a **floating** object:

1. Enable Float with text. This is the default positioning option.

2. Set the Position on text option to set where the object is placed in relation to the artistic text or frame text. Select Left or Right, or set an Indent by value to left-indent by a set pixel value.

3. Once positioned, you can specify the Distance from text: the "standoff" between the object's outline and adjacent text.

4. Click **OK**.

Once attached, the object shows an **Attach to Text** button under the object. Click to edit properties.

The **Attach Point** is a set location in the artistic text or frame text from which the object is positioned from. Drag to a different position in the text to move the attach point and object simultaneously.

Or, for an **inline** object:

1. Enable Position inline as character.

2. To set the object's vertical alignment with respect to adjacent text, select an Align with text option. Text will not flow around the attached object.

3. (Optional) Enter a Offset by value to set the percentage to which the object will be vertically offset in relation to its height.

4. (Optional) Check Scale to to scale the object to a percentage of the adjacent text point size. This keeps the same relative size if the text size changes. Once positioned, you can specify the **Distance from text**: the "standoff" between the object's outline and adjacent text.

4. (Optional) Check **Use these settings when pasting** to update floating and inline defaults. Any subsequent object pasting will adopt the settings saved when the option was checked.

5. Click **OK**. The object appears inline with text, and shows an **Attach to Text** icon.

Objects inserted into text frames use "Float with text" default settings.

To view attached object properties:

1. Select an attached object.

2. Click **Attach to Text** shown under the object.

The **Attached Object Properties** dialog is displayed. The options differ depending on which of the positioning options is enabled. If you'd like to change the position of an attach point you can drag it anywhere else in your text frame. Dragging to an area away from the artistic text/text frame will disconnect your attached object.

To disconnect an attached object:

- From the Attached Object Properties dialog, enable **Detach from text**.

Creating groups

You can easily turn a multiple selection into a group object. When objects are grouped, you can position, resize, or rotate the objects all at the same time.

To create a group from a multiple selection:

- Click the button.

To ungroup (turn a group back into a multiple selection):

- Click the button. The group turns back to a multiple selection.

Simply clicking on any member of a group selects the group object. In general, any operation you carry out on a selected group affects each member of the group. However, the objects that comprise a group are intact, and you can also select and edit an individual object within a group.

To select an individual object within a group:

- **Ctrl**-click the object.

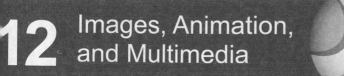

12 Images, Animation, and Multimedia

Adding picture frames

A **picture frame** is a shaped container within which your picture is placed—just like picture frames on the wall at home!

In WebPlus, you can use two types of picture frames, either as:

- **Bordered** picture frames from the Gallery tab.

  - or –

- **Borderless** picture frames from the **Tools** toolbar.

WebPlus lets you import a picture directly into the frame or drag a picture into it from the Media bar. Empty picture frames are shown as envelope-shaped placeholders. At any time you can replace the picture in the frame.

 All selected picture frames that contain a picture will display a supporting Picture frame toolbar under the frame. This offers panning, rotation (90 degrees anti-clockwise), zoom in, zoom out, and replace picture controls).

To add a bordered picture frame:

1. From the Gallery tab, select **Picture Frames** in the drop-down list.

2. Scroll to a sub-category (e.g., Metallic, Natural) of your choice.

3. Drag the frame design thumbnail to your page.

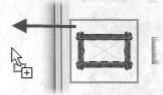

To add a borderless picture frame:

1. For an empty square frame, choose **Picture>Empty Frame...** from the **Insert** menu.

2. The mouse pointer changes to the **Picture Paste** cursor. What you do next determines the initial size and placement of the picture frame.

3. To insert the frame at a default size, simply click the mouse.
   - or -
   To set the size of the frame, drag out a region and release the mouse button.

To add a picture to a frame:

- From the Media bar's currently displayed album, drag and drop a photo directly onto the picture frame.
  - or -

  Click **Replace Picture** directly under the selected frame, locate and select an image. Click **Open**.

The picture is added to the frame using default Picture Frame properties, i.e. it is scaled to maximum fit; aspect ratio is always maintained. However, you can alter the picture's size, orientation and positioning relative to its frame.

To change picture size and positioning:

Select a populated picture frame, and from the accompanying Picture Frame toolbar:

- Click the ▣ button to position the photo in the picture frame by panning.

- Click the ↺ button to rotate the photo in 90 degree anti-clockwise increments.

- Click the ⊕⊖ button to zoom in/out of the photo.

- or -

1. Right-click on a picture frame and choose **Frame Properties...**.
   - or -
   Select the picture frame and choose **Frame Properties** on the Picture context toolbar.

2. In the dialog, you can scale to maximum/minimum, **Stretch to Fit**, or use the original image's size (**No Scale**).

3. To change vertical alignment of pictures within the frames, select **Top**, **Middle**, or **Bottom**.

4. For horizontal alignment, select **Left**, **Centre**, or **Right**.

Importing images

Windows Bitmap (*.bmp)
Windows Enhanced Metafile (*.emf)
Kodak Flash Pix (*.fpx)
Graphic Interchange Format (*.gif)
ICO Decoder (*.ico,*.icon)
Digital Research (*.img)
JPEG 2000 (*.j2k,*.jp2)
JPEG File Interchange Format (*.jpg,*.jpe,*.jpeg)
Kodak Photo CD (*.pcd)
Macintosh PICT (*.pct)
PC PaintBrush (*.pcx)
Portable Network Graphic (*.png)
Adobe Photoshop Image (*.psd)
Paint Shop Pro files (*.psp,*.tub,*.rfr,*.PSPTube)
Sun Raster (*.ras)
Serif Metafile Format (*.smf)
Serif PhotoPlus Picture (*.spp)
Scalable Vector Graphics (*.svg)
Compressed Scalable Vector Graphics (*.svgz)
Targa Bitmap (*.tga)
Tagged Image File Format (*.tif,*.tiff)
Microsoft HD Photo (*.wdp,*.hdp)
Windows Metafile (*.wmf)

WebPlus lets you insert images from a wide variety of file formats.

You can import images from your digital camera or acquire images directly TWAIN-compatible scanners.

Here's a quick overview:

- **Bitmapped** images, also known as **bitmaps** or **raster** images, are built from a matrix of dots ("pixels"), rather like the squares on a sheet of graph paper. They may originate as digital camera photos or scanned images, or be created (or enhanced) with a "paint" program or photo editor. Typical examples include .gif, .jpg, .png, and .wdp.

- **Draw** graphics, also known as **vector** images, are resolution-independent and contain drawing commands such as "draw a line from A to B."

- **Metafiles** are the native graphics format for Windows and combine raster and vector information. Serif also has its own metafile format, Serif MetaFile Format (SMF), which is optimized for image sharing between Serif applications.

Inserting images

There are several ways to bring an image into WebPlus. You can drag a file from an external Windows folder directly onto your page, drag a thumbnail from WebPlus's Media Bar (see p. 261), paste from the pasteboard, or import an image as a file via a dialog.

- **Detached** images float freely on a page, while **inline** images are incorporated with the text flow in a text object.

- **Embedded** images become part of the WebPlus site, while **linking** places a reference copy of the image on the page and preserves a connection to the original file. Each approach has its pros and cons (see Embedding vs. Linking on p. 260).

WebPlus lets you place your image onto the page at its original size. The image will be uncropped by default but you have the option to crop the image, and adjust the image's picture frame properties with respect to image positioning and scaling within the picture frame.

To add an image from the Media Bar:

- Drag an image thumbnail onto the page from the currently displayed album(s) shown in WebPlus's Media Bar (expand the Media Bar from the bottom of your workspace). You can also drag onto an existing image to replace it.

To import an image from a file:

1. (Optional) If you want to place the image inline, click for an insertion point in a text object. For a detached image, make sure text objects are deselected.

2. **In the main window**:

   • Click the 🖾 **Import Picture...** button on the **Standard Objects** toolbar's Picture flyout.
   .

   In WritePlus:
   • Choose **Picture File...** from the **Insert** menu.

3. Use the **Import Picture** dialog to select the image file to open.

4. Select either **Embed Picture** or **Link Picture**. See Embedding vs. linking on p. 260.

5. Click **Open.**

- If there's a text insertion point in the main window, your image will be placed within the text and anchored to the insertion point.

- If you've opened an image via the QuickBuilder Bar, the image will automatically display on the page.

- Otherwise, the mouse pointer will change to the ⊞ **Picture Paste** cursor. What you do next determines the initial size and placement of the detached image.

  - To insert the image at its original pixel size, simply click the mouse.
    - or -
    To set the size of the inserted image, drag out a region and release the mouse button. Use the **Shift** key for unconstrained placement (normal operation is to maintain the image's aspect ratio).

💡 For multi-image pasting, select multiple images in the Open dialog, then paste each image one by one onto the page (by consecutive clicks).

Replacing images

The replace picture option lets you swap an image at any time, especially useful when you want to retain an image's position and dimensions on the page but want to update the image itself. It can be used on any image (uncropped or cropped).

To replace an image:

- Click the 🖼 **Replace Picture** button directly under the selected image, locate and select an image. Click **Open**.

To replace an image via Media Bar:

- Drag an image thumbnail onto an existing image from the currently displayed album(s) shown in WebPlus's Media Bar (expand the Media Bar from the bottom of your workspace first).

Adjusting cropped images

WebPlus provides additional options for working with cropped images—either pictures you've cropped with the Crop tools (Tools toolbar) or replaceable pictures already present in design templates. For example, you can pan or zoom to adjust the portion of the image that displays inside its "frame," or you can change the way the image is scaled and aligned by adjusting its frame properties.

When you select a cropped image with the **Pointer Tool**, a control bar displays below the image, offering panning, rotation, zoom in, zoom out, and replace picture options.

- To reposition a cropped image inside its "frame," click , and then click and drag on the image.

- To rotate an image in 90° anti-clockwise increments, click the button.

- To zoom in or out of an image, click one of the zoom in/out tools.

- To replace an image, click , then browse to locate the new image and click **Open**.

To alter frame properties:

1. Right-click on a cropped image and choose **Frame Properties...**.
   - or -
   Select the image and choose **Frame Properties** on the Picture context toolbar.

2. In the dialog, you can scale to maximum/minimum, **Stretch to Fit**, or use the original image's size (**No Scale**).

3. To change the vertical alignment of the image within the frame, select **Top**, **Middle**, or **Bottom**.

4. For horizontal alignment, select **Left**, **Centre**, or **Right**.

✎ Selecting an uncropped picture offers only a Replace Picture button.

Embedding vs. linking

Embedding means the image in WebPlus is now distinct from the original file. Embedding results in a larger WebPlus file, and if you need to alter an embedded image you'll need to re-import it after editing. Still, it's the best choice if file size isn't an issue and graphics are final.

Linking inserts a copy of the image file into the WebPlus site, linked to the actual file so that any changes you later make to it in the native application will be automatically reflected in WebPlus. Linking is one way of avoiding "bloat" by limiting the size of the site file. On the other hand, you'll need to manage the externally linked files carefully, for example making sure to include them all if you move the WebPlus file to a different drive.

✎ Either option does not affect your published website, only your WebPlus site.

By default, WebPlus prompts you to embed images that are <256 KB, by pre-selecting the "Embed Picture" option in the **Insert** Picture dialog (but you can always select "Link Picture" instead). If you like, you can change the threshold file size or even switch off the automatic selection.

You can check resources via Site Manager later on, to change an item's status from linked to embedded, or vice versa.

For dragging images from the Media Bar, hover over the image thumbnail to check whether it will be embedded or linked when added to the page. To temporarily set the status, hold down the **Ctrl** key to embed the graphic, or the **Shift** key to link the graphic.

To preselect embedding or linking based on file size:

1. Choose **Options...** from the **Tools** menu. Select the **General** menu option.

2. To preselect the "Embed Picture" option for images under a certain size, select the threshold size in the "Embed if smaller than" list. ("Link Picture" will be pre-selected for images larger than the threshold.)

3. To choose whether to embed or link each image, uncheck **Suggest embed/link picture**. You can still select either option in the import dialog; it will now remember and preselect the last setting you used.

Using the Media Bar

The Media Bar acts as a "basket" containing photos for inclusion in your site. Its chief use is to aid the design process by improving efficiency (avoiding having to import photos one by one) and convenience (making photos always-at-hand). For photo-rich websites in particular, perhaps based on a WebPlus design templates, the Media Bar is a valuable tool for dragging photos directly onto unwanted pictures to replace them.

The Media Bar can be used as a temporary storage area before placing photos in your site, or it can be used to create more permanent photo albums from which you can retrieve stored photos at any time. By default, photos are added to a **temporary album** but remember to click the **New Album** button if you want to save your album for later use. Each time you start WebPlus you simply load that saved album (or any other saved album) or just work with a temporary album— the choice is yours!

You can import an unlimited number of photos by file or by whole folders, and whether photos are embedded or linked to your site in advance of photo placement on the page.

For large photo collections, searching throughout albums for photos by file name and EXIF, IPTC or XMP metadata is possible; even edit XMP metadata from within WebPlus.

> The currently loaded album shown on your Media Bar will remain visible irrespective of which site you have open.

Thumbnails can be dragged from the Media Bar directly onto an existing picture on your page, replacing it in the process. Alternatively, a picture can be added as new, being placed at its original size.

To view the Media Bar:

- Unless already displayed, click the ▲ handle at the bottom of your workspace.

To add photos to a temporary album:

1. With the Media Bar visible and a temporary album loaded, click on the Media Bar's workspace to reveal an **Import Picture** dialog.

2. From the dialog, navigate to a folder, then select photo(s) for import.

3. Click **Open**. Your photos appear as thumbnails in the Media Bar workspace.

> Unless you save it, the temporary album and its photo contents will not be saved when you close WebPlus.

You can drag one or more files from any Windows folder directly into the Media Bar window. If you right-click an image in the Media Bar and choose **Locate in Explorer** you'll open the photo's folder via Windows Explorer—great for drag and drop or just general file management!

To save a temporary album to a named album:

1. Click the down arrow on the   **Add To** button. From the menu, select **New Album**.

2. In the **New Album** dialog, in the **Album Name** box, type a name to identify your album in the future.

3. (Optional) For any photo you can alter the embed/link status in advance of placement on your page—click a photo's Placement setting and use the setting's drop-down menu to change. You can also change these settings during drag/drop onto the page.

4. Click **OK**.

To include a temporary album's photos in an existing saved album, click the **Add To** button and choose a named album from the menu.

To create a named album:

1. Click the bar's   **New Album** button.

2. In the dialog, in the **Album Name** box, type a name to identify your album in the future.

3. Click the   **Add Image...** or   **Add Folder...** button.

4. In the dialog, navigate to a photo or folder and click **Open**.

5. The **New Album** dialog lists the files for inclusion. Optionally, alter embed/link Placement option by clicking on each photo's setting, then selecting from the drop-down menu.

6. To delete a photo, select a photo then click the **Remove Image** button.

7. Click **OK**.

To load a saved album:

- Select a saved album name from the bar's top-right drop-down menu. The album's photos will display in the Media bar workspace.

A saved album can be selected as above and then modified via the **Manage** button (only shown for existing saved albums). You can add photos/folders, delete photos, and alter embed/link status.

To delete an album:

- Select an existing album name from the top-right drop-down menu and click **Remove Album**.

To sort results from an album:

- In the **Sort By** search box, choose Filename, Rating, or Date Taken to reorder the photos accordingly to option.

Adding photos to the page

To add a photo to your page:

1. Display the Media Bar's temporary album or load a saved album from the top-right drop-down menu.

2. Drag an album's photo thumbnail onto the page and release your mouse button.

Setting image export options

When you publish your site, WebPlus applies certain global settings to determine how each image—whether drawn, pasted in, or imported—ends up as a separate bitmap displayed on the web page.

Here's a quick summary of the conversion settings as they're initially defined for web publishing:

- Each referenced image is exported as a separate file.

- Any image you inserted as a GIF, JPEG, or PNG is exported as the original file, using its original file name.

- Inserted metafiles and all other graphics are regenerated as PNG images.

You can alter these settings, but before doing so you should review the "logic" WebPlus applies to publishing web graphics. First, WebPlus has one **default format** to which **all** graphics will be converted on export—but you can make exceptions to this rule by specifying that certain image types should remain as their original file. Initially, PNG is the default format, but with **overrides** set for GIFs and JPEGs. That's why, using the initial settings above, PNGs stay as they are while all other graphics get converted to PNGs.

You can check and change these settings in the **Site Properties** dialog (**File** menu). The settings there are global and apply to all graphics in the site—but again you can make exceptions, in this case for individual graphics. To do so, for a selected graphic you could:

- Use the **Export Options...** (**Format** menu) or the **Image Export Manager** (**Tools** menu) to set the export format of particular images on a case-by-case basis.
  - or -
  Convert certain images to a specific format beforehand using the **Tools>Convert to Picture**.

This combination of global and local settings gives you almost total control (if you care to exercise it) over how your graphics make it onto your web pages! Let's look first at how the global settings work.

To set global export options for web graphics:

1. Choose **Site Properties...** from the **File** menu and select the **Graphics** menu option.

2. In the **Export File Format** section, select a preferred export format. This is the default format to which all graphics will be converted on export unless you set overrides. For JPGs, you can set a compression value. For PNGs, **Use PNG transparency** and **Use compatibility hack...** options allow PNG transparency and properly render PNG alpha transparency (in Internet Explorer 5.5 and 6.0), respectively.

3. In the **Resampling** section, choose a resampling method to give Best quality, Good quality, Sharper, or Smoother images of any format; the better quality, the slower the export. Best quality uses **supersampling** to ensure the finest detail in exported graphics. Check the **Don't resample pictures..** option to avoid resampling on images when exported image size will be approximate to original image size.

4. For exporting original graphic file names, in the **Naming** section check **Use original names of picture files**. Graphics will be stored in the root of your published website.

5. In the **Optimization** section, keep **Combine overlapping graphics into a single file** checked to have WebPlus analyze the site and (where a smaller file would result) output overlapping graphics as a single graphic. Whether this option makes sense will depend on your particular layout. Rather than use this global approach, you might consider using **Tools>Convert to Picture** in specific cases.

Setting export options, title, and alternate text for individual graphics

The **Image Export Manager** is a Wizard that lets you set the export file format for individual graphics in the site, or for objects such as rotated text that will be converted to images on export. These local, image-by-image settings **override** the global settings (as set in **File>Site Properties**) which WebPlus uses to determine the export format. You can run the Wizard to check a single selected image, the current page, or the entire site. For each image, you can save it using different methods.

Either:

- Choose a specific format (GIF, JPEG, or PNG) to export to (or just defer to site default settings). For JPEG, you can choose a level of compression.
  - or -

- Save the file to a chosen path and file name on export. Perhaps you want to add more meaningful descriptive names to images on export (especially useful when maintaining your website) instead of having the images export with automatically generated image names.

Let your own eye be the judge. Your best bet is to retain the **Use site default settings** option for all images to start with. Using the original global settings, this means that GIFs, JPEGs, and PNGs will be exported as their original files, while any others, including QuickShapes and closed shapes, will be published as PNGs. Then preview your site and determine if you want to vary the global settings or try a different output format for specific images.

Even if you don't change any format settings, you can set a picture **title** which will normally appear as a tooltip when the image is moused over in a browser. You can also enter **alternate text** (manually or automatically) for accessibility reasons.

To set export format, title, and/or alternate text:

1. If you're checking just a single image, you can select it first and choose **Export Options...** from the **Format** or right-click menu.
   - or -
   To review web export options for images throughout your site, choose **Image Export Manager...** from the **Tools** menu.

2. (Only if you're using the Image Export Manager) Select whether you are checking a selected object, current page or entire site in the Wizard, then click **Continue**. The Wizard cycles through graphics in the specified range, and displays each one in turn along with the Image Export Options dialog.

3. In the dialog's **Save Picture As** section, you can choose to enable either:

   - **Save to a format and name chosen by WebPlus**. The format of the graphic is as defined in Site properties (Graphics; Default Format); the name is generated automatically, e.g. wp479d0ea6.

- **Save in this format with a name chosen by WebPlus**.
  Click a GIF, JPEG, or PNG radio button to specify the export
  format for the current graphic. Enable **Use site default settings** if
  the site's default format is to be maintained but named
  automatically by WebPlus. If selecting JPEG, choose a
  compression quality from the **Compression** drop-down menu.

- **Save to my chosen path and name**.
  Click the **Choose File...** button. The displayed dialog lets you
  export with the original image file name (enable **Use default
  name**) or choose a new image name (enable **Choose name**
  button and enter a new file name). For either method, you can
  navigate to the folder where you want to save the exported image.
  The file format used will be that set in the site default settings.
  You can still override the site default setting by altering the file
  extension in the Choose name field, e.g. change .gif to .png.

4. Check the **Exclude this picture from optimization..** option if you
   don't want the image to be combined into one exported image if
   overlapping with another image in your site.

5. (Optional) Choose from one of several resampling methods—WebPlus
   can resample when needed, the file will always be resampled (e.g.,
   when a JPG is resized) or will never be resampled (original image will
   be used). Enable the appropriate radio button as needed. Changing the
   format will always resample. Resampling can use the quality defined
   in Site Properties (above) or a quality (Best quality, Good quality,
   Sharper, or Smoother) specific to the graphic.

6. To enter a title for a graphic, view the ALT and TITLE tab, and enter
   the appropriate text. This is shown when hovering over an exported
   image.

7. In the same tab, assign an ALT text string to your image for web
   accessibility. The string is read out by screen reader on hover over.
   You can assign text by entry into the input box or you can check **Use
   default ALT text** instead. For the latter, the image is exported as
   follows:

   - If the images is decorative (contains no text) it will have no ALT
     text.
     - or -

- If the image is a clickable graphic such as a labelled button (e.g. Back, Forward, etc.), text on the image is automatically taken, exported as ALT text (i.e., Back, Forward) and presented to a screen reader. If a title graphic is specified, the title text is used as the ALT text.

8. Click **OK**.

Importing TWAIN images

If your scanner or digital camera provides **TWAIN** support, you can scan pictures directly into WebPlus using the TWAIN standard, or save the scanned image and then import into WebPlus.

To set up your TWAIN device for importing:

- See the documentation supplied with your scanner for operating instructions.

To import a scanned image:

- Choose **Picture** from the **Insert** menu, then select **TWAIN** then **Acquire...** from the submenus to open a file selection dialog.

If you have more than one TWAIN-compatible device installed, you may need to select which source you wish to scan with.

To select a different TWAIN source for scanning:

1. Choose **Picture** from the **Insert** menu, then select **TWAIN** then **Select Source...** from the submenu.

2. Identify the device you want to use as your TWAIN source.

Applying PhotoLab filters

Filters can be applied and managed in **PhotoLab**, a powerful studio for applying adjustment and effect filters to pictures individually or in combination—all instantly applied and previewed! PhotoLab offers the following key features:

- **Adjustment filters**
  Apply tonal, colour, lens, and sharpening filters.

- **Effect filters**
  Apply distortion, blur, stylistic, noise, render, artistic and various other effects.

- **Retouching filters**
  Apply red-eye correction, spot repair, straightening, and cropping.

- **Non-destructive operation**
  All filters are applied without affecting the original picture, and can be edited at any point in the future.

- **Powerful filter combinations**
  Create combinations of mixed adjustment, retouching, and effect filters for savable workflows.

- **Selective masking**
  Apply filters to selected regions using masks.

- **Save and manage favourites**
  Save filter combinations to a handy **Favourites** tab.

- **Viewing controls**
  Compare before-and-after previews, with dual- and split-screen controls. Use pan and zoom control for moving around your picture.

- **Locking controls**
  Protect your applied filters from accidental change, then optionally apply them to other images on selection.

PhotoLab hosts filter tabs, a main toolbar, and applied filter stack around a central workspace.

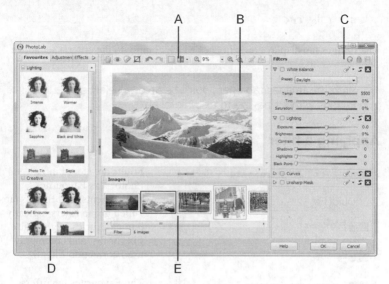

(A) main toolbar, (B) main workspace, (C) filter stack, (D) filter tabs, (E) Images tab

To launch PhotoLab:

1. Select the picture that you want to apply a filter to.

2. Click **PhotoLab** on the Picture context toolbar.

Using the Images tab

Pictures present in your website will show in your **Images** tab (above) if the tab is expanded. This tab is shown by default in PhotoLab but can be hidden by clicking the ▼ button at the bottom of your workspace.

To search site images:

1. Click the **Filter** button on the **Images** tab.

2. Select and define a minimum and maximum image size, if required.

3. Select or deselect RGB, CMYK and Greyscale to show only images in these colour modes.

4. Click **OK**.

The **Images** tab displays only images which comply to the criteria set above.

> With the Images tab open, you'll be able to select and edit all images without having to exit PhotoLab.

Applying a filter

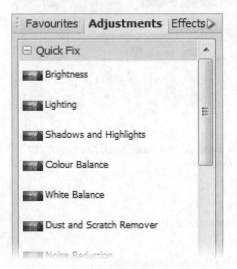

Filters are stored in PhotoLab's Favourites, Adjustments, and Effects tabs which group filters logically into categories (e.g., Quick Fix for fast and commonly used correction filters).

The Favourites tab offers some commonly used filters (individual and in combination). You can complement these with your own user-defined filters.

To apply a filter with trialling:

1. Click a filter thumbnail.

2. As soon as a filter is selected it is temporarily added to **Trial Zone** which lets you experiment freely with your own settings for that filter; the picture automatically refreshes to preview your new settings.

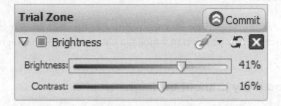

3. Adjust sliders (or enter input values) until your filter suits your requirements. Some filters offer check boxes, drop-down menus, and additional controls (e.g., Advanced settings).

Selecting a new filter always replaces the current filter.

Any filter can be temporarily disabled, reset, or deleted from the trial zone.

To disable: Click ▣, then click ☐ to enable again.

To reset: Click ↩. Any changes to settings are reverted back to the filter's defaults.

To delete: Click ✖.

Once you're sure that you want to keep your filter, you'll need to commit the filter to your filters stack.

To commit your filter:

- Click 🔘 **Commit** to accept your changes. This adds the filter to the right-most **Filters** stack where additional filters can be added and built up by using the same method.

Adjustments are applied such that the most recently added filter always appears at the bottom of the list and is applied to the picture last (after the other filters above it).

To reorder filters:

- Drag and drop your filter into any position in the stack. A dotted line indicates the new position in which the entry will be placed on mouse release.

To add a filter directly (without trialling):

- Click ⊞ **Add Quick Filter** at the top of the Filters stack and choose a filter from the flyout categories. The filter is applied directly to the stack without trialling.

Retouching

PhotoLab offers some useful retouching tools on the main toolbar, each commonly used to correct photos before applying colour correction and effects.

Selective masking

Rather than apply a filter to uniformly change the appearance of your picture, you can change only selected regions instead. PhotoLab lets you mask picture areas by painting areas to be either affected by filters or simply left alone.

To apply a mask:

1. From the ✐ ▾ **Mask** drop-down menu, select **New Mask**.

2. In the Tool Settings pane, select the 🖌️ **Add Region** tool to allow you to mask regions by painting.

3. Adjust the settings to suit requirements, especially adjusting Brush Size to paint larger or more intricate regions.

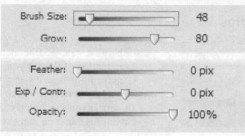

Change the **Mode** drop-down menu from Select to Protect to protect painted regions from masking (i.e., the inverse of the Add Region option).

4. Using the on-screen cursor, paint regions (in green for adding; red for protecting).

   🖌️ If you've not been as accurate as you'd like while painting, you can click **Remove Regions** then paint over the unwanted painted regions.

5. Click ✔️ **Accept** to save your masking changes.

The mask button changes to yellow when a mask is applied.

It's also possible to create additional masks for the same filter as above, and then choose between masks accordingly. You can only have one mask applied at any one time. By using the menu's **New From>** option you can also base the new mask on another mask applied to the current or any other filter in the filter stack. This is useful when using favourites containing multiple adjustments.

To edit a mask:

- Click the down arrow on the  button, choose the mask name and select **Edit Mask**.

Saving favourites

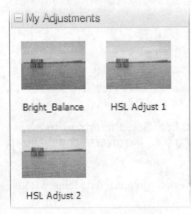

If there's a specific filter setting (or combination of filters) you want to keep for future use it's easy to save it as a **favourite**. PhotoLab stores all your favourites together in the Favourites tab. You can even create your own categories (e.g. My Adjustments) within the tab.

To save filter(s) as a new favourite:

- Click 🖫 **Save Filter**.

- From the dialog, enter a favourite name and pick a category to save the filter to. (Click ⸬ to create new category)

▽ If you want to further manage your favourites into user-defined categories, click the option on the **Tab Menu**.

Using Image Cutout Studio

Image Cutout Studio offers a powerful integrated solution for cutting objects out from their backgrounds. Depending on the make up of your images you can separate subject of interests from their backgrounds, either by retaining the subject of interest (usually people, objects, etc.) or removing a simple uniform background (e.g., sky, studio backdrop). In both instances, the resulting "cutout" image creates an eye-catching look for your site.

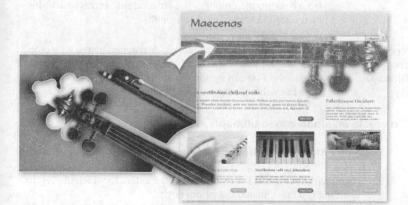

To launch Image Cutout Studio:

1. Select an image to be cut out.

2. Select **Image Cutout Studio** from the displayed Picture context toolbar. Image Cutout Studio is launched.

Choose an output

It's essential that you choose an output type prior to selecting areas for keeping/discarding. Either an alpha-edged or vector-cropped bitmap can be chosen as your output type prior to selection. The choice you make really depends on the image, in particular how well defined image edges are.

> Zoom into your image to examine its edges; this may influence the output type chosen.

Let's look at the output types and explain the difference between each.

Output Type	Description and use
Alpha-edged Bitmap	Use when cutting out objects with poorly defined edges. Transparency and pixel blending are used at the outline edge to produce professional results with negligible interference from background colours. The term "alpha" refers to a 32-bit image's alpha transparency channel.
Vector-cropped Bitmap	Use on more well-defined edges. A cropped image wi.h crop outline is created which can be later manipulated with the crop tools. You can optionally apply feathering to the image edge but will not remove background colour.

To create an alpha-edged bitmap:

1. Select **Alpha-edged Bitmap** from the **Output Type** drop-down menu.

2. (Optional) Drag the **Width** slider to set the extent to which the "alpha" blending is applied inside the cutout edge.

3. (Optional) Adjust the **Blur** slider to smooth out the cutout edge.

To create a vector-cropped bitmap:

1. Select **Vector-cropped Bitmap** from the **Output Type** drop-down menu.

2. (Optional) Drag the **Feather** slider to apply a soft or blurry edge inside the cutout edge.

3. (Optional) Drag the **Smoothness** slider to smooth out the cutout edge.

4. (Optional) The **Inflate** slider acts as a positive or negative offset from the cutout edge.

You'll need to click 　 **Preview** in order to check output setting adjustments each time.

Selecting areas to keep or discard

A pair of brushes for keeping and discarding is used to "paint" areas of the image. The tools are called **Keep Brush** and **Discard Brush**, and are either used independently or, more typically, in combination with each other. When using either tool, the brush paints an area contained by an outline which is considered to be discarded or retained (depending on brush type). A configurable number of pixels adjacent to the outline area are blended.

To aid the selection operation, several display modes are available to show selection.

Show Original, **Show Tinted**, and **Show Transparent** buttons respectively display the image with:

- selection areas only

- various coloured tints aiding complex selection operations

- checkerboard transparency areas marked for discarding.

For **Show Tinted**, a red tint indicates areas to be discarded; a green tint shows areas to be kept.

Background Colour

For **Show Transparent** mode, a different **Background colour** can be set (at bottom of the Studio) which might help differentiate areas to keep or discard.

To select image areas for keeping/discarding:

1. In Image Cutout Studio, click either **Keep brush** or **Discard brush** from the left of the Studio workspace.

2. (Optional) Pick a **Brush size** suitable for the area to be worked on.

48 pix

3. (Optional) Set a **Grow tolerance** value to automatically expand the selected area under the cursor (by detecting colours similar to those within the current selection). The greater the value the more the selected area will grow. Uncheck the option to switch the feature off.

4. Using the circular cursor, click and drag across the area to be retained or discarded (depending on Keep or Discard Brush Tool selection). It's OK to repeatedly click and drag until your selection area is made.

The **Undo** button reverts to the last made selection.

To fine-tune your selection, you can switch between Keep and Discard brushes by temporarily holding down the **Alt** key.

5. If you're outputting an alpha-edged bitmap, you can refine the area to be kept/discarded within Image Cutout Studio (only after previewing) with Erase and Restore touch-up tools. Vector-cropped images can be cropped using standard WebPlus crop tools outside of the Studio.

Make your outline edge as exact as possible by using brush and touch-up tools before committing your work.

Click **Reset** if you want to revert your selected areas and start your cutout again.

6. Click **OK** to create your cutout.

You'll see your image on the site page in its original location, but with the selected areas cut away (made transparent).

Refining your cutout area (alpha-edged bitmaps only)

If a vector-cropped image is created via Image Cutout Studio it's possible to subsequently manipulate the crop outline using crop tools. However, for alpha-edged bitmaps, Erase and Restore touch-up tools can be used to refine the cutout area within the Studio before completing your cutout. The latter can't be edited with crop tools.

The touch-up tools are brush based and are only to be used to fine-tune your almost complete cutout—use your Keep and Discard brush tools for the bulk of your work!

To restore or remove portions of your cutout:

1. With your cutout areas already defined, click 🔘 **Preview** (Output settings tab). You can use the button to check your cutout as you progress.

2. Click the ✏️ **Restore Touch-up Tool** or 🖌️ **Erase Touch-up Tool** button from the left of the Studio workspace.

3. Paint the areas for restoring or erasing as you would with the brush tools.

4. Click **Ok**.

If you've touched up part of your image between each preview, you'll be asked if you want to save or discard changes.

Adding animation

WebPlus lets you add several varieties of eye-catching animation effects to any web page: **animated marquees**, **GIF animations** (see WebPlus Help), and **Flash** (SWF) files. For any of the animation effects, you can preview the animation and/or customize the effect. Once placed into your site, the animations appear static, but they will spring to life once the site has been exported and a visitor views your page in a web browser.

Animated marquees

Animated marquees are an impressive way to add horizontally scrolling motion to a headline or catch phrase. You can choose the background colour, enter from one to three lines of text, define text properties (choose from any installed font), scroll direction, speed and alignment for each line. If you like, you can define any link destination type for the marquee (see Adding hyperlinks and anchors on p. 85). For the most compelling effect, select two lines with strongly contrasting text colours and opposing scroll directions.

Animated marquees appear as static graphics on the WebPlus page. You can cut, copy, move, and resize them just like other graphics. They will animate when previewed or viewed in a web browser.

To create an animated marquee:

- Click the 📇 **Insert Animated Marquee** button on the **Web Objects** toolbar's Media flyout.

To edit an animated marquee you've already defined:

- Double-click the marquee. The Insert Animated Marquee dialog redisplays, with the current settings in place.

Flash files

A Flash (*.swf) file is a viewable movie using the Flash™ Player format. (Flash is a vector-based program designed to create and display small files on the web.) Flash files can be added to your page (much like an image) and will play within your page view without the need for previewing in your browser (or WebPlus preview window). You can cut, copy, move, and resize them just like other graphics.

To see some Flash files in action, the Gallery tab hosts a stunning collection of Flash banners (each with pre-assigned Flash parameters already set) which can be easily adopted. These banners are designed to allow you to customize their appearance (i.e., text, images, and scheme colours) without any prior Flash design experience.

To insert a Flash file:

1. Click the 🎬 **Insert Flash file** button on the **Web Objects** toolbar's Media flyout.

2. Use the dialog to select the Flash file to open (click **Browse...** then select your SWF file). Click **Export Options** to optionally define a different file name and/or file location. To keep the animation separate from the WebPlus file (using a link to the source file) uncheck **Embed files in site**.

3. (Optional) In the **Parameters** window, click the **Add...** (or **Edit**) button to add (or edit) parameters as name/value pairs.

4. (Optional) In the **Additional Files** window, build up a library of files (e.g., images) which are used to make up your Flash movie. Think of it as a local library in which supporting files are easily at hand and easily referenced. Click the **Add...** button to navigate to then select files for addition (use Ctrl-click or Shift-click for contiguous or non-contiguous file selection, respectively).

5. (Optional) The Display box controls how the Flash movie is presented on your WebPlus page. Experiment with the options for different looping, transparency, alignment, scaling, and quality options.

6. Click **OK**.

7. You'll see the ⊞ Picture Paste cursor. Click to insert the file at a default size or drag to set a custom size region.

To edit a Flash banner:

1. Double-click your Flash movie.

2. (Optional) Change **Export Options...** and whether you want to embed the file in your WebPlus site.

3. In the Parameters box select any parameter **Name** in the list and click the **Edit** button (you don't need to use the **Add...** button when editing Flash banners). Depending on the Flash banner chosen, you can edit several types of parameter value, i.e.

- Text values can be changed from their placeholder text, e.g. a placeholder text value for "line 1" can be overwritten with your own text (e.g., "Say it.."). You can equally use a token as a replacement value (e.g. a token of *%companyname%* will automatically show the company name set in User Details in your banner—in this case "Flowers-2-Go").

- Scheme values can be altered by again editing token values, e.g. to use your site's scheme colour 2 instead or scheme colour 1 you can edit %scheme1% to be %scheme2%.

- Parameter values for pictures work slightly differently to text and schemes. Each picture that makes up your banner is referenced in the parameters list, e.g. Pic1URL, Pic2URL, and Pic3URL represents the first, second and third pictures listed in the **Additional Files** list. You can either reorder pictures in the Additional Files list (**not** the Parameters list) using the **Up** or **Down** buttons to make pictures appear in a different sequence or use the right-most **Add...** button to add new files to the Additional Files list to replace currently referenced pictures. There's no need to edit the Parameter values at all—the key is to set the pictures and their order in the Additional Files list only.

Remember to remove any unwanted pictures from the Additional Files list.

4. (Optional) Uncheck **Embed files in site** if you don't want additional files to be embedded in your site.

5. (Optional) The Display box controls how the Flash movie is presented on your WebPlus page. Experiment with the options for different looping, transparency, alignment, scaling, and quality options.

6. Click **OK**.

The selected Flash banner is shown with any previously made edits applied.

If you experience any playback problems when Flash files are placed on your page, it is possible to uncheck **Preview Flash objects** in **Tools>Options** (Layout menu). Exported web pages containing Flash files are unaffected.

Adding sound and video

WebPlus lets you augment your web pages with sound and video files in a variety of standard formats, including both **non-streaming** and **streaming** media. In addition, WebPlus lets you include third-party videos already hosted on www.youtube.com.

Sound

- There are actually two sound playback options—**background sound**, where a sound loads and plays automatically when a specific page is first displayed in the visitor's web browser, and **linked sound**, triggered by a mouse click (for example, on an icon or hyperlinked object). The supported audio formats are AIFF, AU, MIDI (.mid, .midi), MP3, RealAudio (.ra, .ram), and WAV.

Video

- **Linked video** works like linked sound. Supported video formats are AVI, QuickTime (.mov, .qt), MPEG (.mpg, .mpeg, .mpe, .mpv), and RealVideo (.ram, .rv). (Non-streaming files must download in entirety to a user's computer before they begin playing; streaming files require a special player that buffers incoming data and can start playing before the whole clip has arrived.)

- **YouTube videos** which are already published on the Internet can be included on your web page. Videos themselves are not embedded in your site; instead, just the unique YouTube video ID is embedded in your page as you place the YouTube video on your page—a link is created from your web page back to www.youtube.com. This lets you add media content to your pages while avoiding uploading large videos as part of your site.

With both background and linked sound (or video), you have the option of **embedding** the source file in your site, as opposed to keeping it separate (remember that YouTube videos cannot be embedded in your site).

To add background sound to a page:

1. Right-click the page in the workspace and choose **Page Properties...**.

2. From the **Effects** tab, check **Use sound file**, then from the Open dialog, browse and select to the sound file you want to add. Click **OK**.

3. If you do **not** wish to embed the file, uncheck **Embed sound file in site**.

4. To have the sound play back as a continuous loop, check **Loop sound**. Otherwise, it will play just once.

5. (Optional) Set **Export Options...** to define an exported file name and physical location. (See Setting image export options on p. 265.)

6. Click **OK**.

The sound file will download and play back when the web page displays in a browser.

The basic question is how you want the visitor to be able to trigger the playback of a given media file. WebPlus offers the same basic options for both kinds of media:

- **From a hyperlinked object (or hotspot):** You start with an existing object in the site, and hyperlink it to the media file, or use a hotspot over an image.

- **From a video thumbnail preview**: You click on an embedded video thumbnail which commences video playback (YouTube videos only).

- **From an icon:** WebPlus provides an icon pre-linked to the media file. You then position the icon on your page.

- **From a picture:** You select an external picture file, which WebPlus then imports and links to the media file.

- **Inline:** A media "player" will be visible on your published web page (rather than appearing after the user clicks a link, icon, or picture). In WebPlus, you'll see a marker on the page where the player will appear.

With the first two options, the media file remains external and can't be embedded in your site. Options 3 to 5 give you the choice of embedding the media file.

To add linked sound or video to an object or hotspot:

1. Select the object or hotspot and choose **Hyperlink** from the **Tools** toolbar.

2. In the dialog, select **File** to create a hyperlink to a sound file on your hard disk.

3. Click **Browse**, locate and select the media file, and click **Open**.

4. If you do **not** wish to embed the file, uncheck the **Embed picture file in site** option.

5. (Optional) Set **Export Options...** to define an exported file name and physical location. (See Setting image export options on p. 265.)

6. A range of target windows or frames can be chosen depending on how you want the link destination to be displayed. (See Adding hyperlinks and anchors on p. 85.).

7. Click **OK**.

To embed a YouTube video:

1. Open the www.youtube.com website in your browser, and choose the YouTube video that you want to link to.

2. Copy the URL address for the video (or embed code). This contains an alphanumeric ID, e.g. ySnp4YXU6JQ, which uniquely identifies the video clip.

3. Click the **Insert YouTube Video** button on the **Web Objects** toolbar's Media flyout.

4. From the dialog, paste the video URL into the input box.

5. (Optional) Check/Uncheck the boxes to enable/disable the following;

    - **Autoplay**
      Automatically plays the video once the page has loaded.

    - **Loop**
      Continuously plays the video.

    - **Show video info**
      Displays the title and star rating of the video.

    - **Allow full screen mode**
      Adds a button to the video window so that the user can opt to
      view the video in full screen mode.

    - **Include related videos**
      (If **Loop** is checked, the **Include related videos** feature is
      automatically disabled. If you want to enable this feature, you
      will need to clear the Loop check box.) At the end of the video,
      displays recommended videos related in content to the current
      video playing on your page. Also displays a search bar so that
      users can browse and play other videos from YouTube on your
      site.

    - **Play in HD**
      Plays the video in High-Definition, if the video itself has been
      created for High-Definition playback.

    - **Show Border**
      Adds a border around the video window. Click the two buttons to
      access drop-down palettes and select up to two colours.

6. Click **OK**. Position the ▨ **Paste** cursor where you want the top-
    left corner of your video to be placed.

7. To insert the video at a default size, simply click the mouse.
    - or -
    To set the size of the inserted video, drag out the cursor and release the
    mouse button. The video resizing will be unconstrained but you can
    maintain the video's aspect ratio by pressing the **Shift** key as you drag.

Some websites may require their YouTube video(s) to be swapped for another on an occasional or more regular basis. For example, the site may host a regularly changing top 10 or videos with topical content. Either way, WebPlus can replace videos without affecting their placement.

To swap your YouTube video for another, double-click an existing YouTube video. From the dialog, paste a previously copied video URL into the input box.

To link from an icon, picture, or inline player:

1. Click the ♫ **Insert Sound Clip** or ▦ **Insert Video Clip** button on the **Web Objects** toolbar's Media flyout.

2. Browse to locate the media file name.

3. If you do **not** wish to embed the file, uncheck the **Embed picture file in site** option.

4. Select a link display option (icon, inline, or picture).

5. Click **OK** to close the dialog, then click (or click and drag) with the cursor to place the icon, picture, or marker on your page.

Using the Photo Gallery

The simultaneous expansion of digital camera usage and Broadband services has created a fantastic opportunity for publishing photo collections on web pages. There are a multitude of reasons for doing so but some common ones include:

- hosting family photos for access by geographically distant relatives

- Special occasions (parties, Christmas, meetings, holidays)

- cataloguing collections (e.g., of animals, stamps, etc.)

In WebPlus you can add a Flash™- or JavaScript-based photo gallery to any web page. By using the power of Flash you can also adopt some eye-catching gallery styles, each offering different ways of cycling through photos. Photo galleries let you navigate via a top or bottom control bar or, depending on gallery style, by using:

- thumbnail rollovers (opposite)

- vertical thumbnails

- photo grids

- photo stacks

- lightboxes

Photos can be imported by file or folder, or from a TWAIN device (digital camera/scanner). By default, large photos imported into the gallery are automatically resized and exported at the maximum resolution of 720 x 540 pixels. If photos are smaller than 720 x 540 pixels, they will remain unchanged.

During import, you have the option to manage multiple selected photos simultaneously.

- Reorder your photos into your preferred display order.

- Perform bulk editing. You'll be able to caption, rotate*, and adjust brightness, and contrast.

- Assign Exif tags and create custom captions.

- Create and manage photo albums.

*Automatic rotation of digital camera photos (landscape to portrait) is possible (if supported by camera).

Creating the Gallery

The Photo Gallery is inserted on the page, just like an individual photo, after collecting your photos together from file, folder, camera, or scanner.

> ✎ All the photos are output as JPGs regardless of the original photo type and the settings in **File>Site Properties>Graphics**.

To insert a Photo Gallery:

1. Click the 🖼 **Insert Photo Gallery** button on the **Standard Objects** toolbar's Picture flyout.

2. (Optional) Click **Advanced** to change default photo size and quality settings.

3. Select the type of photo gallery you want to use;

    - **Professional Flash Photo Gallery**
      (Visitors to your site will require Flash 9 and above.)

    - **Flash Photo Gallery**
      (Visitors to your site will require Flash 8 and above.)

    - **JavaScript Photo Gallery**

4. Click **Next**. From the dialog, choose whether to:

    - **Add individual files**
      Click the **Add Files** button to navigate to then select the photo file(s) to open. Use **Ctrl**-click or **Shift**-click to select multiple non-adjacent or adjacent files. Use the **Preview** window to examine the photos as you add to your current selection.

    - or -

    - **Add all photos in a folder**
      Click the **Add Folder** button to navigate to a folder then select it to add its contents.

    - or -

- **Add from a digital camera or scanner**
  Click the **Add TWAIN** button.

- To delete one or all thumbnails, select and click the **Delete** button.

Your photos display as thumbnails in the **Photo Gallery** dialog.

5. (Optional) Select one or more gallery thumbnails for manipulation;

- To adjust photo order, use the ⬆ **Up** and ⬇ **Down** buttons at the bottom of the dialog.
  - or -
  Click ➡ **Move to position** and input a position number.

- To rotate in 90° clockwise intervals, click the ↻ **Rotate** button.
  - or -
  Click the **Rotate right** column and select a rotation increment from the drop-down.

- To add a caption, click the **Caption** column and input text, numbers and characters.

- ⟨⟩ To create captions from Exif, IPTC and XMP photo tags, click **Format captions**. Select a tag type from the drop-down and then click **Add Tag**. A preview will display in the **Caption Preview** box. Select where to add the captions—**Add to start of caption**, **Add to end of caption** or **Overwrite caption**. Click **OK**.

- To find and replace captions, click 🔍 **Find caption**. (See the topic Using find and replace on p. 200.)

- To adjust **Brightness** and **Contrast**, click the respective columns and input values between 0 and 100.

- To replace a photo, right-click the selected photo and then click **Replace image**.

- (Professional Flash Photo Gallery only) To organize photos into albums, click **Edit albums**. Check the **Enable albums within gallery** box and select the number of albums you want to use, up to a maximum of 24. Give your album(s) a **Title**, **Description** and optionally assign **Background music** to play while the album is running in the gallery. Click **OK**.

- (Professional Flash Photo Gallery only) To add hyperlinks to photos, click 📇 **Edit hyperlink**. From the dialog, choose a **Hyperlink Type**—you can set no hyperlink, hyperlinks to the original image, or hyperlinks to a different link destination (e.g., Site Page or Internet Page). For the last option you have to double-click the No link text to choose the link destination.

6. To include selected photos within your site, check **Embed Images**. By default, photos are kept separate from the WebPlus file (using a link to the source file).

7. Click **Next**.

8. Select a Gallery style from the **Gallery Style** pane running across the top of the dialog. Each type offers a different style for photo navigation.

9. (Optional) For the selected style, use the pane on the right to modify various gallery-wide options (accompanying background music, font colour, AutoPlay, etc.).

10. Click **Finish**.

11. ▦ To insert the gallery at a default size, position the displayed cursor where you want the gallery to appear on the page, then simply click the mouse.
    - or -
    To set the size of the inserted gallery, drag out a region and release the mouse button.

Editing the Photo Gallery

Once added to the web page, the Photo Gallery can be edited. Photos can be added, removed, rotated, captioned, or adjusted using Brightness and Contrast settings. You can also swap your existing gallery style for another, change photo hyperlinks, background music, caption text colour, and set your gallery to autoplay (photos will automatically cycle).

> ⚲ If you have several galleries within your site, you can manage previously set hyperlinks from the Hyperlink option in Site Manager. Choose **Gallery Image** from the **Type** drop-down menu.

To edit a Photo Gallery:

1. Select a gallery already present on your web page.

2. Double-click the gallery.

   The Photo Gallery dialog is displayed. The options available are the same as those available when the gallery was created.

Linking remote images

It is possible to connect to any image currently available on the Internet. However, to prevent copyright infringement it's advisable to use images from a reliable image hosting service. Of course you may be able to "hotlink" to other images (from a friend or colleague's site) where legal implications are not an issue but it's only polite to **ask for permission first**!

To insert a remote image:

1. Go to **Insert>Picture>Remote link...**.

2. In the dialog, enter the absolute URL for the image.

3. Click **OK**.

4. You'll see the mouse pointer change to the ▦ Picture Paste cursor. What you do next determines the initial size and placement of the image.

5. To insert the image at a default size, simply click the mouse.
   - or -
   To set the size of the inserted image, drag out a region and release the mouse button.

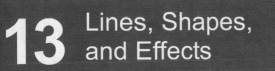

13 Lines, Shapes, and Effects

Drawing and editing lines

WebPlus provides **Pencil**, **Straight Line**, and **Pen** tools for drawing freehand, straight, and curved/straight lines, respectively.

The  **Pencil Tool** lets you sketch curved lines and shapes in a **freeform** way.

The **Straight Line Tool** is for drawing **straight** lines; rules at the top and/or bottom of the page; or horizontal lines to separate sections or highlight headlines.

The **Pen Tool** lets you join a series of line segments (which may be **curved** or **straight**) using "connect the dots" mouse clicks.

Any curved line can be closed (by joining line ends) to create a custom **shape** (see Drawing and editing shapes on p. 303 for details)

Drawing lines

To draw a freeform line (with the Pencil Tool):

1. Click the ![pencil icon] **Pencil Tool** from the **Standard Objects** toolbar's Line flyout.

2. Click where you want the line to start, and hold the mouse button down as you draw. The line appears immediately and follows your mouse movements.

3. To end the line, release the mouse button. The line will automatically smooth out using a minimal number of nodes.

4. To extend the line, position the cursor over one of its red end nodes. The cursor changes to include a plus symbol. Click on the node and drag to add a new line segment.

To draw a straight line (with the Straight Line Tool):

1. Click the ![line icon] **Straight Line Tool** from the **Standard Objects** toolbar's Line flyout.

2. Click where you want the line to start, and drag to the end point. The line appears immediately.

> To constrain the angle of the straight line to 15° increments, hold down the **Shift** key as you drag. (This is an easy way to make exactly vertical or horizontal lines.)

3. To extend the line, position the cursor over one of its red end nodes. The cursor changes to include a plus symbol. Click on the node and drag to add a new line segment.

To draw one or more line segments (with the Pen Tool):

1. Click the ![pen icon] **Pen Tool** from the **Standard Objects** toolbar's Line flyout. On the Curve context toolbar, three buttons let you select which kind of segment to draw:

A **Straight** segment is simply a straight line connecting two nodes. (**Shortcut:** Press **1**)

A **Bézier** segment is curved, displaying control handles for precise adjustment. (**Shortcut:** Press **2**)

Smart segments appear without visible control handles, using automatic curve-fitting to connect each node. They are especially useful when tracing around curved objects and pictures. (**Shortcut:** Press **3**)

2. Select a segment type, then click where you want the line to start.

- For a **Straight** segment, click again (or drag) for a new node where you want the segment to end. **Shift**-click to align the segment at 15° intervals (useful for quick right-angle junctions).

- For a **Bézier** segment, click again for a new node and drag out a **control handle** from it. Control handles act like "magnets," pulling the curve into shape. The distance between handles determines the depth of the resulting new curved line segment.

    Click again where you want the segment to end, and a curved segment appears. The finished segment becomes selectable.

- For a **Smart** segment, click again for a new node. The segment appears as a smooth, best-fitting curve (without visible control handles) between the new node and the preceding node. Before releasing the mouse button, you can drag to "flex" the line as if bending a piece of wire. If the preceding corner node on the line is also smart, flexibility extends back to the preceding segment. You can **Shift**-click to create a new node that lines up at 15° intervals with the previous node.

3.   To extend an existing line, repeat Step 2 for each new segment. Each segment can be of a different type.

4.   To end the line, press **Esc**, double-click, or choose a different tool.

Editing lines

Use the Pointer Tool in conjunction with the Curve context toolbar to adjust lines once you've drawn them. The techniques are the same whether you're editing a separate line object or the outline of a closed shape.

When selected, each line type shows square nodes which can be used for reshaping lines.

See WebPlus help for information on editing lines.

Setting line properties

All lines, including those that enclose shapes, have numerous properties, including colour, weight (width or thickness), scaling, cap (end), join (corner), and stroke alignment. You can vary these properties for any freehand, straight, or curved line, as well as for the outline of a shape. Text frames, pictures, tables, and artistic text objects have line properties, too.

In WebPlus, you can control the position of the stroke (i.e., line width) in relation to the object's path, i.e. the line that defines the boundary of the object.

To change line properties of a selected object:

- Use the Swatches tab to change the line's colour and/or shade. Alternatively, use the Colour tab to apply a colour to the selected object from a colour mixer.

  The object's line and fill can take a solid or gradient colour, as well as bitmaps and transparency effects.

- Use the Line tab, context toolbar (shown when a line is selected), or Line and Border dialog to change the line's weight (thickness), type, or other properties. Select a line width, and use the drop-down boxes to pick the type of line.

On the Line tab, context toolbar, or Line and Border dialog, the styles drop-down menu provides the following styles: **None**, **Single**, **Calligraphic**, and several **Dashed** and **Double** line styles as illustrated below.

Several techniques offer additional ways to customize lines:

For dotted/dashed lines, select from one of five line styles (see above).
- or -
(tab and dialog only) Drag the **Dash Pattern** slider to set the overall pattern length (the number of boxes to the left of the slider) and the dash length (the number of those boxes that are black).

The illustrations below show lines with dash lengths of (**1**) 4 and 2, and (**2**) 5 and 4:

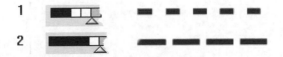

1

2

For double lines, select from one of four **Double** line styles (see above).

(Tab only) For calligraphic lines of variable width (drawn as if with a square-tipped pen held at a certain angle), select the calligraphic line style (opposite) from the drop-down menu, then use the **Calligraphic Angle** box to set the angle of the pen tip, as depicted in the examples below.

You can also vary a line's **Cap** (end) and the **Join** (corner) where two lines intersect.

The Line and Border dialog offers all line properties including Edge Selection options, shading/tinting, line end scaling, plus decorative photo-based borders for framing photos.

To access all Line properties:

•   Click the ⤢ **Line/Border** button on the **Tools** toolbar's Fill flyout..

In the dialog, the **Line** tab lets you adjust all line properties (detailed above) while the **Border** tab provides photo-based borders.

Drawing and editing shapes

QuickShapes are pre-designed objects of widely varying shapes that you can instantly add to your page.

Once you've drawn a QuickShape, you can morph its original shape using control handles, and adjust its properties—for example, by applying solid/gradient colours, bitmaps (including your own bitmap pictures!), and transparency effects to both the object's outline and fill.

Another way to create a shape is to draw a line (or series of line segments) and then connect its start and end nodes, creating a closed shape.

QuickShapes

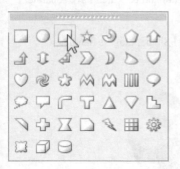

The QuickShape flyout on the **Standard Objects** toolbar contains a wide variety of commonly used shapes, including boxes, ovals, arrows, polygons, stars, cubes, and cylinders.

Once added to the page, it's also possible to use the QuickShape context toolbar situated above the workspace to adjust your QuickShape's line weight, colour, style, and more.

New shapes always take the default line and fill (initially a black line with no fill).

To create a QuickShape:

1. Click the 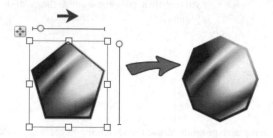 **QuickShape** flyout on the **Standard Objects** toolbar and select a shape.

2. Click on the page to create a new shape at a default size.
    - or -

    Drag across the page to size your shape. When the shape is the right size, release the mouse button.

To draw a constrained shape (such as a circle):

• Hold down the **Shift** key as you drag.

All QuickShapes can be positioned, resized, rotated, and filled. What's more, you can morph them using adjustable sliding handles around the QuickShape. Each shape changes in a logical way to allow its exact appearance to be altered.

To adjust the appearance of a QuickShape:

1. Click on the QuickShape to reveal one or more sliding handles around the shape. These are distinct from the "inner" selection handles. Different QuickShapes have different handles which have separate functions.

2. To change the appearance of a QuickShape, drag its handles.

Closed shapes

As soon as you draw or select a line, you'll see the line's nodes appear. Nodes show the end points of each segment in the line. Freehand curves typically have many nodes; straight or curved line segments have only two. You can make a shape by drawing a line back to its starting point.

To turn a selected line into a shape:

- Select the line with the Pointer Tool and click the  **Close Curve** button on the Curve context toolbar.

You can go the other way, too—break open a shape in order to add one or more line segments.

To break open a shape:

1. Select the node where you want to break the shape.

2. Click the **Break Curve** button on the Curve context toolbar.

3. You can now use the Pointer Tool to reshape the line as needed.

Editing shapes

- Use the **Weight** slider in the **Line tab** to change the weight (thickness) or type of the shape's border. For a different line style (dotted, dashed, etc.), click the middle drop-down list to apply it.

- Use the **Colour** tab or **Swatches** tab to change the shape's line or fill colour (solid, gradient or bitmap).

- Use the **Transparency** tab to apply gradient or bitmap transparency.

Using 2D filter effects

WebPlus provides a variety of **filter effects** that you can use to transform any object. "3D" filter effects let you create the impression of a textured surface and are covered elsewhere (see p. 310). Here we'll look at 2D filter effects exclusively. The following examples show each 2D filter effect when applied to the letter "A."

Drop Shadow

Inner Shadow

Outer Glow

Inner Glow

Inner Bevel

Outer Bevel

Emboss

Pillow Emboss

Gaussian Blur

Zoom Blur

Radial Blur

Motion Blur

Colour Fill

Feather

Outline

Reflection

The Studio's Styles tab offers a range of 2D filter effects that are ready to use. Its multiple categories each offer a gallery full of predefined effects, such as shadows, bevels, reflections, blurs, and more. Each category offers subtle variations of the category effect. Click any thumbnail to apply the effect to the selected object.

WebPlus additionally provides the Shadow Tool for applying a shadow to an object directly on your web page. Control handles let you adjust shadow blur, opacity and colour.

For absolute control over your 2D filter effects, you can use fx **Filter Effects**.

To apply 2D filter effects:

1. Select an object and click the fx **Filter Effects** button on the **Tools** toolbar's Effects flyout.

2. To apply a particular effect, check its box in the list at left.

3. To adjust the properties of a specific effect, select its name and vary the dialog controls. Adjust the sliders or enter specific values to vary the combined effect. (You can also select a slider and use the keyboard arrows.) Options differ from one effect to another.

4. Click **OK** to apply the effect to the selected object, or **Cancel** to abandon changes.

Creating reflections

A simple way to add creative flair to your page is to apply a vertical reflection on a selected object. The effect is especially eye-catching when applied to pictures, but can be equally impressive on artistic text, such as page titles or text banners. A combination of settings can control reflection height, opacity, offset and blurring.

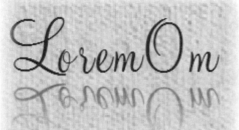

Creating outlines

WebPlus lets you create a coloured outline around objects, especially text and shapes (as a **filter effect**). For any outline, you can set the outline width, colour fill, transparency, and blend mode. The outline can also take a gradient fill, a unique **contour** fill (fill runs from the inner to outer edge of the outline width), or pattern fill and can also sit inside, outside, or be centred on the object edge.

As with all effects you can switch the outline effect on and off. You'll be able to apply a combination of 2D or 3D filter effects along with your outline, by checking other options in the Filter Effects dialog.

Using the Shadow Tool

Shadows are great for adding flair and dimension to your work, particularly to pictures, text objects, and shapes. To help you create them quickly and easily, WebPlus provides the **Shadow Tool** on the **Tools** toolbar's Effects flyout. The tool affords freeform control of the shadow effect allowing creation of adjustable **basic** or **skewed edge-based shadows** for any WebPlus object.

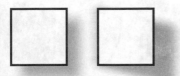

*Basic (left) and skewed shadows
(right) applied to a square
QuickShape.*

Adjustment of shadow colour, opacity, blur, and scaling/distance is possible using controllable nodes directly on the page (or via a supporting Shadow context toolbar). Nodes can be dragged inwards or outwards from the shadow origin to modify the shadow's blur and opacity. For a different colour, select the Colour node then pick a new colour from the Colour or Swatches tab. Depending on if a basic or skewed shadow is required, the origin can exist in the centre (shown below) or at the edge of an object, respectively.

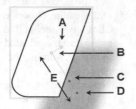

(A) Blur, (B) Shadow origin, (C) Opacity, (D) Colour, (E) Scaling

Once you've created a shadow, you can also fine-tune it as needed using the Filter Effects dialog.

Using 3D filter effects

3D filter effects go beyond 2D filter effects (such as shadow, glow, bevel, and emboss effects) to create the impression of a textured surface on the object itself. You can use the **Filter Effects** dialog to apply one or more effects to the same object. Keep in mind that none of these 3D effects will "do" anything to an unfilled object—you'll need to have a fill there to see the difference they make!

The Studio's Styles tab is a good place to begin experimenting with 3D filter effects. Its multiple categories each offers a gallery full of pre-defined mixed 2D and 3D effects, using various settings.

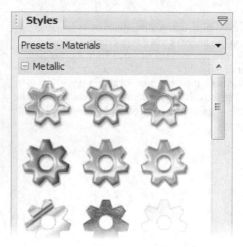

There you'll see a variety of remarkable 3D surface and texture presets in various categories (Presets - Default, Presets - Fun, Presets - Materials, and Texture). The Presets - Materials category offers realistic effects such as Glass, Metallic, Wood, etc. Click any thumbnail to apply it to the selected object. Assuming the object has some colour on it to start with, you'll see an instant result!

fx Alternatively, you can customize a Styles tab preset, or apply one or more specific effects from scratch, by using **Filter Effects**.

To apply 3D filter effects:

1. Click 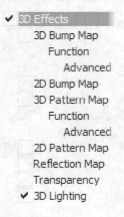 **Filter Effects** on the **Tools** toolbar's Effects flyout.

2. Check the **3D Effects** box at the left. The **3D Lighting** box is checked by default.

> ✔ 3D Effects
> 　　3D Bump Map
> 　　　Function
> 　　　　Advanced
> 　　2D Bump Map
> 　　3D Pattern Map
> 　　　Function
> 　　　　Advanced
> 　　2D Pattern Map
> 　　Reflection Map
> 　　Transparency
> ✔ 3D Lighting

3. Adjust the "master control" sliders here to vary the overall properties of any individual 3D effects you select.

   - **Blur** specifies the amount of smoothing applied. Larger blur sizes give the impression of broader, more gradual changes in height.

   - **Depth** specifies how steep the changes in depth appear.

   - The ⊞ button is normally down, which links the two sliders so that sharp changes in Depth are smoothed out by the Blur parameter. To adjust the sliders independently, click the button so it's up.

4. Check a 3D effect in the 3D Effects list and experiment with the available settings.

Using object styles

Object styles benefit your design efforts in much the same way as text styles and colour schemes. Once you've come up with a set of attributes that you like—properties like line colour, fill, border, and so on—you can save this cluster of attributes as a named style. WebPlus remembers which objects are using that style, and the style appears in the **Styles tab**, and can subsequently be applied to new objects. For example a Quick Star can have a glass effect applied via an object style you've saved previously (all object styles use a cog shape as the default object preview type).

Here's how object styles work to your advantage:

- Each object style can include settings for a host of object attributes, such as line colour, line style, fill, transparency, filter effects, font, and border. The freedom to include or exclude certain attributes, and the nearly unlimited range of choices for each attribute, makes this a powerful tool in the designer's arsenal.

- Any time you want to alter some aspect of the style (for example, change the line colour), you simply change the style definition. Instantly, all objects in your site sharing that style update accordingly.

- Object styles you've saved globally appear not only in the original site but in any new site, so you can reuse exactly the same attractive combination of attributes for any subsequent design effort.

The Styles tab contains multiple galleries of pre-designed styles that you can apply to any object, or customize to suit your own taste! Galleries exist in effect categories such as Blurs, 3D, Edge, Warps, Shadows, Materials (e.g., metals) and more, with each category having further subcategories.

To apply an object style to one or more objects:

1. Display the **Styles** tab.

2. Expand the drop-down list to select a named style category (e.g., Blurs), then pick a subcategory by scrolling the lower window.

3. Preview available styles as thumbnails (cog shapes are shown by default) in the window.

4. Click a style thumbnail to apply it to the selected object(s).

To remove an object style from a gallery:

- Right-click the thumbnail and choose **Delete**.

To unlink an object from its style definition:

- Right-click the object and choose **Format>Object Style>Unlink**.

If you've applied a style to an object but have lost track of the thumbnail—or want to confirm which style is actually being used on an object—you can quickly locate the thumbnail from the object.

To locate an object's style in the Styles tab:

- Right-click the object and choose **Format>Object Style>Locate in Studio**.

The Styles tab displays the gallery thumbnail for the object's style.

Normally, a site's object styles are just stored locally—that is, as part of that site; they don't automatically carry over to new sites. If you've created a new style you'll want to use in another site, you can save it globally so that it will appear in the Styles tab each time you open a new site.

Saving Object Styles

To create a new object style based on an existing object's attributes:

1. Right-click the object and choose **Format>Object Style>Create**.

2. The Style Attributes Editor dialog appears, with a tree listing object attributes on the left and a preview region on the right (not shown).

3. Click to expand or collapse sections within the attributes tree. Check any attributes you want to include in the style definition, and uncheck any you don't want to include.

4. If you want to change any of the current object settings, double-click an attribute (or select it and click the **Edit** button). This will bring up a detailed dialog for the particular attribute.

5. The **Object** pane in the preview region shows the currently selected object after applying the defined style. Select the **Artistic Text** or **Frame Text** tab to see the style applied to sample objects of those types.

6. Click the **Browse...** button to select the gallery category where you want to locate the style thumbnail, and optionally, save to a different Preview Type (Rounded Rectangle, Frame Text, or Artistic Text) instead of the default cog shape.

7. Type a name to identify the gallery thumbnail.

8. Click **OK**. A thumbnail for the new object style appears in the designated gallery.

Once an object style is listed in a gallery, you can modify it or create a copy (for example, to define a derivative style) by right-clicking on its thumbnail and choosing **Edit...** or **Copy...**.

To save a site's object styles globally:

1. Choose **Save Defaults...** from the **Tools** menu.

2. From the dialog, check **Object styles**, then click **Save**.

Adding dimensionality (Instant 3D)

Using the **Instant 3D** feature, you can easily transform flat shapes (shown) and text into three-dimensional objects.

WebPlus provides control over 3D effect settings such as bevelling, lighting, lathe effects, texture, and material control.

An always-at-hand 3D context toolbar hosted above your workspace lets you configure the above settings—each setting contributes to the 3D effect applied to the selected object. For on-the-page object control you can transform in 3D with use of a red orbit circle, which acts as an axis from which you can rotate around the X-, Y-, and Z-axes in relation to your page.

Look for the cursor changing as you hover over the red circles' nodes or wire frame.

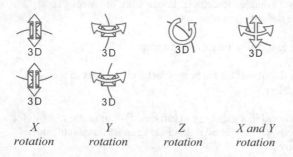

X	*Y*	*Z*	*X and Y*
rotation	*rotation*	*rotation*	*rotation*

> Transform about your 3D objects' axes instead of your pages' axes by holding the **Ctrl** key down as you transform.

You can also adjust the angle and elevation of each "active" light on the page by dragging the light pointer to a position which simulates a light source.

To add dimensionality:

1. Select an object and click the **Instant 3D** button from the **Tools** toolbar's Effects flyout. The object immediately adopts 3D characteristics with a red orbit circle displayed in the object's foreground.

2. Click a 3D effect category from the first drop-down menu on the 3D context toolbar; the bar's options change dynamically according to the category currently selected. See the online Help for more details.

To switch off 3D effects:

*   Click the **Remove 3D** button on the context toolbar.

To edit base properties of a 3D object:

*   Select the 3D object, then click the **Edit Base Object** button at the bottom right-hand corner of the 3D object.

The original object's shape is shown, allowing its selection handles to be manipulated for resizing and rotating.

14 Colour, Fills, and Transparency

Applying solid colours

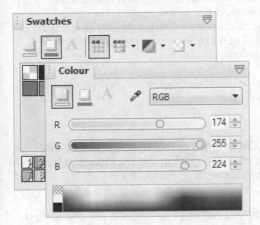

You can use the Colour tab, Swatches tab or a dialog box to apply solid colours to an object.

The tabs' swatch buttons offer a number of ways to apply solid colours to objects of different kinds:

- You can apply solid colours to an object's **fill** or **line**. As you might expect, QuickShapes and closed shapes (see Drawing and editing shapes on p. 303) have both line and fill properties.

- **Freehand** or **curved lines** can take **line** colours but also a **fill** colour for creating closed shapes directly from the line.

- Selected **artistic** and **Creative frame text objects** can take a background fill, line, and a text colour. The text colour is the fill of the text, the background fill is the area immediately behind the text. HTML frame text only takes a background fill and text colour.

- **Text frames** (shown) and **table cells** can have a background fill independent of the characters they contain.

To apply a solid colour via the Colour tab:

1. Select the object(s) or highlight a range of text.

2. Click the **Colour** tab and select one of several colour modes (RGB, CMYK, HSL, or Greyscale) from the drop-down list.

3. Click the ⬜ **Fill** or ⬜ **Line**, or **A** **Text** button at the top of the tab to determine where colour will be applied. The colour of the underline reflects the colour of your selected object. For selected frame text, the Fill will be the background text colour (but not the frame's background colour).

4. Select a colour from the colour spectrum or sliders depending on colour mode selected.

☿ Why not use the 🖊 **Colour Picker** tool to define the **colour**?. After choosing the tool, click anywhere in the workspace to "pick up" the colour under the cursor.

☿ ▽ In RGB colour mode, you can use hexadecimal colour coding by selection from the Colour tab's **Tab Menu** button.

To apply a solid colour via the Swatches tab:

1. Select the object(s) or highlight a range of text.

2. Click the **Swatches** tab.

3. Click the ⬜ **Fill** or ⬜ **Line**, or **A** **Text** button at the top of the tab to determine where colour will be applied.

4. ▦ ▦▾ Select a colour swatch from the **Site Palette** (commonly used colours and those previously applied in your site) or standard **Palette** (standard RGB or themed palette presets such as WebSafe colours).

Alternatively, use **Format>Fill...** to apply colour via a dialog.

To change a solid colour's shade/tint (lightness):

1. Select the object and set the correct Fill, Line or Text button in the Colour tab.

2. From the Colour mode drop-down menu, select **Tinting**.

3.   Drag the Shade/Tint slider to the left or right to darken or lighten your starting colour, respectively. You can also enter a percentage value in the box (entering 0 in the input box reverts to the original colour).

Object tinting can also be applied via the Swatches tab—adjust `0%` **Tint** via slider or direct input.

 WebPlus automatically adds used colours to the   **Site Palette** in the Swatches tab.

To change the current palette:

*   Click the   **Palette** button to view and adopt colours from a standard RGB, WebSafe, or selection of themed palettes. Colours can be added, edited or deleted from the Site Palette but not from other palettes.

Using colour schemes

WebPlus offers an impressive selection of **colour schemes** that can be selected when creating a site using a design template or from scratch. If you choose a template-based site, the selection of a colour scheme will set the look and feel of your site with respect to colour, as all templates are already "schemed". Selecting each scheme dramatically changes the colours of page elements in your page layout with just one click!

When you initially create your site from a template you can select either one of three colour schemes designed specifically for that template design, or just use any of the global colour schemes. See Creating a site using a design template on p. 20.

Creating schemes from scratch

Websites created from scratch can use any global colour scheme—but you'll have to initially assign scheme colour to objects (see p. 321) as they are created to make colour scheming work. This will allow dramatic colour change if you subsequently change schemes.

How colour schemes work

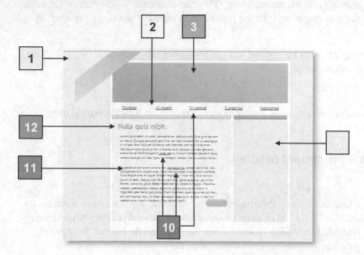

Colour schemes in WebPlus work much like a paint-by-numbers system, where page elements in a layout are assigned specific scheme **colours** by number.

These colours are stored in "paint jar" swatches, numbered 1 to 12, hosted on the Swatches tab.

Smoothie colour scheme

These swatches represent the **site colour scheme**. From here, you can assign scheme colours to page elements to make them schemed (this process is done already with templates).

Swapping to a different colour scheme produces an completely different look with respect to colour.

What happened to numbers 4 and 6 to 9 above? These were not needed in the page layout and therefore weren't assigned.

You can use a theme layout design template to get an idea of how scheme colours could be assigned to different page elements in your site. The table opposite indicates how page elements are mapped to swatch colours (from the scheme called Smoothie).

Swatch #	Description
1	Site Background
2	Main Container
3	Header
4	Main Panel
5	Sidebar
6	Colour Variation 1
7	Colour Variation 2
8	Badge
9	Button
10	Text - Hyperlinks
11	Text - html
12	Text - Headings

Try swapping between different schemes by using the "Schemes - Sample" sample file available initially from WebPlus's Startup Wizard or **File** menu. Load the file and swap between colour schemes via the **Colour Scheme Designer**.

Schemed hyperlinks, page colours, and backgrounds

Any one of the 12 scheme colours can also be used for hyperlinks, on-page colour, and the site background for your site.

For hyperlinks in particular, the normal, followed, active, and rollover hyperlink states are schemed by default. They all adopt the same Scheme Colour 10 as shown above, but by assigning different scheme colours in Site properties (p. 32) you can make the hyperlink colour change on different types of interactivity (click, hover over, etc.).

On-page colours are not schemed by default, but can be assigned a colour scheme in Site properties at any time. Conversely, site backgrounds are schemed to colour swatch 1 by default, but can be swapped for another scheme colour at any time.

For more details about setting page colour and site background colour, see Setting page appearance on p. 35.

Other ways of using scheme colours

Heading 1
Heading 2
Heading 3

Text styles, just like other objects, can be assigned scheme colours. This is especially useful if you'd like your headings to adopt a similar appearance. Of course you can change the scheme at any time, updating all your heading colours immediately.

See Setting text properties and Using text styles on p. 203 and p. 205.

Heading 1 - link
Nulla quis nibh. Proin ac pede vel ligula facilisis gravida. *Phasellus* purus. Etiam sapien. Duis diam urna, iaculis ut, vehicula ac, varius sit amet, mi. Donec id nisl.

Heading 2 - link
Aliquam erat volutpat. *Integer fringilla*. Duis lobortis, quam non volutpat suscipit, magna sem consequat libero, ac hendrerit urna ante id mi. Quisque

Different schemed colours can also be applied to hyperlinks on text styles throughout your site. This may be useful if you wish to distinguish hyperlink colours used on headings (e.g. Heading 1, Heading 2) from those used on Body text.

Selecting colour schemes

To select a preset colour scheme:

1. Click 🌐 **Colour Scheme Designer** on the default context toolbar.

   - or -

   Display the **Swatches** tab, to show the current colour scheme, e.g.

   Click the ⋅⋅ button.

2. From the dialog's Colour Schemes tab, double-click a different colour scheme sample from the list (or select and click **Load**), then click **OK**.

Any regions in the site that have been assigned one of the twelve colour scheme numbers are updated with the corresponding colour from the new scheme.

Each site can have just one colour scheme active at any one time; this is called the **site colour scheme** and is always shown in the Swatches tab. When you save a site, its current colour scheme is saved along with the site.

> The **Colour Scheme Designer** also lets you modify scheme colours and even create your own custom colour schemes.

Applying scheme colours to objects

If you create new objects in a web template site, or start a site from scratch, how can you extend a colour scheme to the new objects? Although you'll need to spend some time working out which colour combinations look best, the mechanics of the process are simple. All you need to do is assign one of the scheme colour numbers to an object's line and/or fill.

To assign a scheme colour to an object:

1. Select the object and choose a **Fill**, **Line**, or **A** **Text** button at the top of the Swatches tab depending on the desired effect.

2. From the bottom of the Swatches tab, click on a scheme colour that you want to apply to the fill, line and text (or you can drag the colour instead).

If an object's fill uses a scheme colour, the corresponding sample in Swatches tab will be highlighted whenever the object is selected.

Modifying colour schemes

If you've tried various colour schemes but haven't found one that's quite right, you can modify any of the colours in an existing scheme.

To modify a colour scheme:

1. Click **Colour Scheme Designer** on the default context toolbar.

2. From the Colour Schemes tab, select the scheme to modify (double-click a scheme or select and click **Load**).

3. From the dialog, each of the scheme colour numbers has its own drop-down menu, showing available colours in the WebPlus palette.

   Click the scheme colour's drop-down arrow and select a colour from the menu (or click **More Colours...** for more colour choice).

Colour Scheme:

Scheme Colour 1	▼
Scheme Colour 2	▼
Scheme Colour 3	▼
Scheme Colour 4	▼
Scheme Colour 5	▼
Scheme Colour 6	▼
Scheme Colour 7	▼

Sea Green

More Colours...

The scheme is updated with the new colour. Repeat to modify other scheme colours.

4. To apply the scheme to the current site, click **OK**. The site colour scheme is now updated.

> Schemes that have been modified are stored with the site, although custom colour schemes can also be saved globally, so the full set of schemes is always available to new sites.

> To create a new named scheme based on these colours, click **Save As**. Alternatively, use **Save** to overwrite the existing scheme.

For more advanced colour scheme design using suggested colour combinations, see online Help.

Working with gradient and bitmap fills

Gradient fills provide a gradation or spectrum of colours spreading between two or more points on an object. A gradient fill has an editable path with nodes that mark the origin of each of these key colours. A bitmap fill uses a named bitmap—often a material, pattern, or background image—to fill an object.

| *Linear* | *Elliptical* | *Conical* | *Bitmap* |

You can apply preset gradient and bitmap fills from the Swatches tab to the fill or outline of a shape or text frame; artistic text can also take a gradient or bitmap fill (for the text, its outline, and background).

Creative frame text and creative table text can also have gradient or bitmap fills applied (for the text, outline, and background), along with individual creative table cell borders and backgrounds.

Applying different transparency effects (using the Transparency tab) won't alter the object's fill settings as such, but may significantly alter a fill's actual appearance.

Applying a gradient or bitmap fill

There are several ways to apply a gradient or bitmap fill: using the Swatches tab, Fill Tool, or a dialog.

The easiest way to apply a gradient or bitmap fill is to use one of a range of pre-supplied swatch thumbnails in the Swatches tab's **Gradient** or **Bitmap** palettes. The Fill Tool and a Fill dialog are alternative methods for creating gradient fills (these are covered in online Help).

To apply a gradient or bitmap fill using the Swatches tab:

1. Click the Swatches tab and ensure either the ▬ **Fill** or ▬ **Line** is selected (for an object's fill or outline, respectively).
   Note that the colour of the underline reflects the colour of your selected object.

2. For gradient fills, select Linear, Elliptical or Conical as the gradient type from the **Gradient** button's drop-down menu.
   - or -
   For bitmap fills, select a drop-down menu category from the **Bitmap** button.

3. Select the object(s), and click the appropriate gallery swatch for the fill you want to apply.
   - or -

   For fills only, drag from the gallery swatch onto any object and release the mouse button.

4. If needed, adjust the fill's **Tint** at the bottom of the tab with the tab slider or set a percentage value in the input box.

To apply a gradient fill with the Fill Tool:

1. Select an object.

2. Click the ◇ **Fill Tool** button on the **Tools** toolbar's Fill flyout.

3. Click and drag on the object to define the fill path. The object takes a simple Linear fill, grading from the object's current colour to monochrome white, e.g.

If the object is white already (or has no fill), grading is from white to black.

Editing the fill path

When you select a fillable object, the **Fill Tool** becomes available (otherwise it's greyed out). If the object uses a **gradient fill**, you'll see the **fill path** displayed as a line when the Fill Tool is selected. Nodes mark where the spectrum between each key colour begins and ends. Adjusting the node positions determines the actual spread of colours between nodes. You can also edit a gradient fill by adding, deleting, or changing key colours.

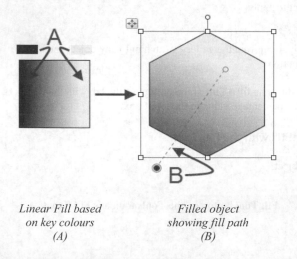

Linear Fill based
on key colours
(A)

Filled object
showing fill path
(B)

To adjust the gradient fill path on a selected object:

1. Display the Swatches tab and ensure either  **Fill** or **Line** is selected (for an object's fill or outline, respectively).

2. Click the **Fill Tool** button on the **Tools** toolbar's Fill flyout. The fill path appears on the object's fill or outline.

3. Use the Fill Tool to drag the start and end path nodes, or click on the object for a new start node and drag out a new fill path. The gradient starts where you place the start node, and ends where you place the end node.

Each gradient fill type has a characteristic path. For example, Linear fills have single-line paths, while Radial fills have a two-line path so you can adjust the fill's extent in two directions away from the centre. If the object uses a **bitmap fill**, you'll see the fill path displayed as two lines joined at a centre point. Nodes mark the fill's centre and edges.

Setting transparency

Transparency effects are great for highlights, shading and shadows, and simulating "rendered" realism. They can make the critical difference between flat-looking illustrations and images with depth and snap. WebPlus fully supports variable transparency and lets you apply solid, gradient, or bitmap transparencies easily.

For example, in the illustration below, the butterflies have a solid (100% opaque) transparency, a gradient (100% to 0% opaque) transparency and a solid (50% opaque) transparency from left to right.

Transparencies work rather like fills that use "disappearing ink" instead of colour. The more transparency in a particular spot, the more "disappearing" takes place there, and the more the object(s) underneath show through. Just as a gradient fill can vary from light to dark, a transparency can vary from more to less, i.e. from clear to opaque, as in the illustration:

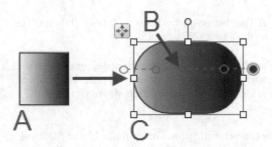

A - Linear Transparency, B - Path, C - Effect on Object

In WebPlus, transparency effects work very much like greyscale fills. Just like fills...

- Transparency effects are applied from the Studio—in this case, using the Transparency tab via solid, gradient, and bitmap galleries.

- The Transparency tab's gallery has thumbnails in shades of grey, where the lighter portions represent more transparency. To apply transparency, you click thumbnails or drag them onto objects.

- Most transparency effects have a path you can edit—in this case, with the Transparency Tool.

Transparency types available in the Transparency tab are as follows:

- **Solid** transparency distributes the transparency uniformly.

- **Gradient** transparencies include linear, elliptical, and conical effects (each thumbnail's tooltip identifies its category), ranging from clear to opaque.

- **Bitmap** transparencies include categorized texture maps based on the Swatches tab's selection of bitmaps.

Applying transparency

You can apply gradient and bitmap transparency from the Transparency tab to the fill or outline of a shape or text frame; artistic text can also use the same transparency effects (for the text, its outline, and background).

To apply transparency with Transparency tab:

1. With your object selected, display the Transparency tab and ensure

    either ⬜ **Fill** or ⬜ **Line** is selected (for an object's fill or outline, respectively).

2. For solid transparency, select the ⬜ **Solid** button and pick a thumbnail from the solid transparency gallery. The lighter thumbnails represent more transparency (expressed as percentage Opacity).
    - or -

    For gradient transparency, choose the ◢ **Gradient** button and pick your thumbnail.
    - or -

    For bitmap transparency, choose the ▦ ▾ **Bitmap** button and pick a thumbnail from a range of categories.

3. The transparency is applied to the object's fill or outline.

Alternatively, drag the desired thumbnail from the gallery to an object, and release the mouse button.

To apply gradient transparency with Transparency Tool:

1. Select the object and set the Transparency tab's Fill/Line swatch as before.

2. Click the 🍸 **Transparency Tool** button on the **Tools** toolbar's Transparency flyout.
   - or -
   Select **Format>Transparency...**.

3. Drag your cursor across the object and release the mouse button. The object takes a simple Linear transparency, grading from 100% opacity to 0% opacity (fully transparent).

Setting the default transparency

The **default transparency** means the transparency that will be applied to the next new object you create. Local defaults only affect objects in the current site. For information on setting defaults in WebPlus, see Updating and saving defaults on p. 241.

15 Previewing
and Publishing

Previewing your site

Previewing your site in a web browser is an essential step before publishing it to the web. It's the only way you can see just how your site will appear to a visitor. You can **preview** a page or site at any time, either within WebPlus (using an internal window based on the Internet Explorer browser) or separately using any browser installed on your system.

To preview your site:

1. Click the down arrow on the 🖳 ▾ **Preview site** button on the **Standard** toolbar.

2. Select an option from the submenu:

    *   **Preview in Window** (shortcut **Alt+P**) opens the site in a new internal WebPlus window with its own tab for convenient switching.

        When previewing in a window, you can use the Preview context toolbar to control the preview window. Click the toolbar buttons to navigate **Back** and **Forward**, **Refresh** or **Close Preview**, and redisplay the page at one of several standard or custom screen resolutions (all from a drop-down menu).

    *   Choose **Preview Page...** or **Preview Site...** to use an external browser. The names will reflect which browsers are currently installed, e.g. the entry may read "Preview Page in Internet Explorer." If you have more than one browser installed, you can select which browser(s) to display on the submenu. The page or site is exported to a temporary folder and appears in the specified browser.

To customize the list of browsers on the submenu:

1. Choose **Preview Site** from the **File** menu (or from the Preview Site flyout on the **Standard** toolbar) and select **Browser Preview List...** from the submenu.

    The dialog displays a list of browsers registered on your system. The WebPlus **Preview** submenu will list these in the order they're shown here.

2. Use the dialog to make changes as needed:

- Click **Auto Detect** to refresh the list automatically, or click **Add** to display a dialog that lets you locate a particular browser to manually add to the list.

- To delete an entry from the list, select it and click **Remove**.

- You can rearrange the list by selecting an entry and clicking **Move Up** or **Move Down**.

- To change the entry's name on the submenu or its path, select the entry and click **Edit**. For example, you could change "Internet Explorer" to appear as simply "IE7".

3. Click **OK** to confirm any changes.

It is good practise to install several of the common browsers in order to test how your site will look on an alternative system.

WebPlus allows you to view estimated download time for each page of your site, and provides information such as the number of files on each page and the total size of the files. This is carried out via the **Standard** toolbar's **Preview Site** flyout.

Publishing to the web

Publishing to the web involves uploading your site to your web host provider, turning your site into a live website, viewable by the whole world! You can specify that all web pages are published or, if updating your site, only pages changed since the last "publish."

Before publishing to the web, it is worth checking for potential problems by running the Site Checker (**Tools>Site Manager>Site Checker...**).

Remember that you can publish to disk folder at any time, which lets you test your website offline (and locally) before publishing to web. See WebPlus Help for more details.

To publish your site to the web:

1. Choose **Site Properties...** from the **File** menu and double-check export settings, particularly those viewable from the Graphics menu option.

2. Click the ⬛ ▾ **Publish site** button on the **Standard** toolbar (or choose **Publish Site** from the **File** menu and select **Publish to Web...** from the submenu).

If you've not set up FTP account information, you'll need to set up at least one account before you can proceed—this will be remembered for subsequent web publishing.

3. Click the **Accounts...** button to display the **Upload to Server** dialog.

4. Click **Add...**

5. In the **Account Details** dialog, enter:

   - The **Account name**. This can be any name of your choice. You'll use it to identify this account in WebPlus (in case you have more than one).

   - The **FTP address** of your web host will be a specific URL starting with "ftp://" as supplied by your service provider.

   - **Port number**: Unless directed by your provider, you can leave this set at "21."

   - Leave the **Folder** box blank unless directed by your provider, or if you want to publish to a specific subfolder of your root directory.

   - You'll also need a **Username** and **Password** as pre-assigned by the provider. Most likely these will correspond to email login settings. Be sure to enter the password exactly as given to you, using correct upper- and lower-case spelling, or the host server may not recognize it.

   - Check **Save password** to record the password on your computer, if you don't want to re-enter it with each upload.

- **Passive mode**: Leave checked unless you have FTP connection problems (check with your ISP). ISPs can operate passive or active FTP modes of operation.

- **Web site URL**: Set your site's URL. This allows you to view the web site from a dialog after FTP upload.

- In the **Advanced** box, you can optionally enable Secure FTP by uploading using one of two encryption protocols—TLS 1.0 and SSL 3.0. Check **Encrypt connection**, then choose the **Protocol**. You'll need to confirm with your ISP whether encryption (and which protocol) is supported, implied or otherwise. The **SSL Implied** option makes the ISP's FTP server encrypt on initial contact to default port 990 or a custom port (edit Port number).

- Click **OK** to close Account Details.

You can also use the Upload to Server dialog at this point to **Add...** another account, and **Copy...**, **Edit** or **Delete** an account selected from the drop-down menu. It's a good idea to test your new or modified account by clicking the **Test** button—if the test is successful a dialog will display stating that a connection has been established.

> If you add additional accounts you'll need to select which account to use from the drop-down list in the FTP Account box.

You can choose to Save FTP account details either to your machine (account details will be saved into WebPlus and won't be lost, even after Ctrl-Runup) or into the current site.

6. If you've set up at least one account and clicked the **Update Account...** button, the **Publish to Web** dialog appears with the last used account name shown in the drop-down menu and its settings in subsequent boxes. The drop-down menu lets you swap to another account. Select the account you want to use (if you've more than one).

7. If your site is using a database, the **Merge before publishing** option is checked. Clear this option only if you do not wish to merge changes (the option will be greyed out if no database/changes are detected). For more on databases, see Using database merge in WebPlus Help.

8. For the greatest control over the publishing, ensure that the **Unattended upload** check box is cleared. This will allow you to

review the changes that will take place to your published website before they are made. It will also give you the option to cancel the upload if you discover a problem. (See Automatic Operation on p. 343 for more details on this feature.)

9. Choose which pages you want to upload—check specific page(s) in the window or **Publish All Pages**. Use the **Toggle Select**, **Toggle Branch** and **Select All** buttons to aid page selection.

10. To safeguard your WebPlus site, check the **Backup the document to the remote server** option. If the site is unsaved you'll be prompted to save it.

11. Click **OK**. WebPlus seeks an Internet connection, then:

12. If uploading for the first time, selected files will be uploaded directly.
    - or -

    If uploading to an existing site, an Uploading Files dialog is displayed showing local file action (whether files will be added (Add), will replace the live file (Replace) or not updated (Leave)).

    In the dialog, check the option to Delete unused remote files if you want WebPlus to automatically remove any unused graphic and page files.

    Select either the **Incremental Update** or **Full upload** Button. Choose the former to upload only files that have altered since the last upload. When doing an incremental update, you can get WebPlus to **Check for missing files** by checking the option box. However, as this can dramatically slow the upload, this option is unchecked by default.

    You'll see a message when all files have been successfully copied. Click **Close**.

13. From the drop-down menu in the Website Publishing dialog, select the browser in which you wish to view your live site and click **View this URL**. You will now be able to view your live site.

If you rename/delete files and then republish one or a few pages to the web, the old files are not deleted automatically so you'll need to delete these manually by using **Publish Site>Maintain Website...** on the **File** Menu. However, if you republish the whole site to the web automatically (using Automatic Operation), you can choose to delete any unused files; check the **Delete unused files** check box.

Handling FTP account information

WebPlus gives you the option of saving your FTP account details either on your machine or in the current site, or both. Account details are kept on the computer by default, but by saving details within your site you can transfer your site to another machine without losing your account details and then republish from there.

> Password details are never stored in sites for security reasons.

An additional option allows you to export **all** FTP account details (including passwords) onto a different computer.

To save FTP account details in your site:

1. From the **Publish to Web** dialog, click **Accounts...**.

2. In the dialog's Save FTP account details section, check **Into current site**.

3. Click **Update Account**.

When the site is opened on another machine, the details will still only be stored on the site. You can optionally check the **On this machine** option to store the account details on the machine as well as in the site.

To export all FTP account details:

1. From the **Publish to Web** dialog, click **Accounts...**.

2. In the dialog's FTP Account section, click **Export All**.

3. Choose a location and file name for the registry file (.reg), then click **Save**.

4. Transfer the .reg file to a different computer, then double-click the file.

> Any existing FTP accounts on the target computer will be overwritten.

Automatic Operation

If you have a very large website, you may want to use the Automatic Operation feature. The actual process is virtually the same as Publish to Web but it allows you to upload the site without having to "OK" each dialog that may appear. This is especially useful if you are updating a site containing a large database with images.

1. Check **Unattended upload.** This also enables the following options;

    *   Check **Use incremental upload** to only replace files that have changed from the last upload (if you've already published the website to the same FTP folder previously), which is an efficient method of uploading since there are less files to transfer.

        With this enabled you can also select **Check remote files** to prompt WebPlus to manually check each file before replacing it. This decreases the speed of uploading compared to normal operation but is a more thorough method of publishing.

    *   Check **Delete unused files** to remove files from the FTP folder that aren't needed for the website you are publishing (e.g., this is relevant when you upload a completely different website to your FTP folder).

2. Choose which pages you want to upload—check specific page(s) in the window or **Publish All Pages**. Use the **Toggle Select**, **Toggle Branch** and **Select All** buttons to aid page selection.

3. To safeguard your site, check the **Backup the document to the remote server** option. If the site is unsaved you'll be prompted to save it.

4. Click **OK** to begin the upload process. (Now is the time to get that cup of tea...)

5. Once the upload is complete, the Uploading files dialog will remain on screen until you click **Close**.

6. From the drop-down menu in the Website Publishing dialog, select the browser in which you wish to view your live site and click **View this URL**. You will now be able to view your live site.

Viewing your published site

Once your site has been published, you have the option to ⚙ **View Site Online** from the 🖥 ▾ **Preview site** drop-down menu on the **Standard** toolbar. This displays your site in its most recently published state in the default web browser. The first time View site online is used, a dialog pops up asking for the default site URL. This can be amended later using the **Site Properties...** dialog.

It is important to remember that any changes made since publishing will not be reflected. To see unpublished changes, use the 🖥 ▾ **Preview site** button. (See Previewing your site on p. 337.)

Setting up your web space

Serif provides competitively priced web hosting that offers various levels of service to suit your individual requirements. See http://go.serif.com/hosting for more details.

Quick Publish

Quick Publish allows you to quickly upload and view the currently displayed page—useful for live verification of individual pages as you build your website. In order for Quick Publish to function, you must first setup your account details using the Quick Publish Configuration dialog.

To configure Quick Publish:

1. Click the 📷 ▾ **Publish site** flyout on the **Standard** toolbar and then click **Quick Publish Configure**.

    - or -

    Click **File>Publish Site>Quick Publish Configuration...**

2. In the dialog:

    - Enter the details of, or select from the drop-down menu, the URL of the site you want to publish to.

    - Select the browser in which you wish to view your page once it has been published.

    - Select the FTP account you want to use from the drop-down menu. To update account settings, or add a new account, click **Manage Accounts**.

    It's a good idea to test your new or modified account by clicking the **Test** button—if the test is successful a dialog will display stating that a connection has been established.

3. Click **OK**.

To Quick Publish to Web:

- Click the ⬛ ▾ **Publish site** flyout on the **Standard** toolbar and then click **Quick Publish to Web**.

    - or -

    Click **File>Publish Site>Quick Publish to Web.**

> If you attempt to use Quick Publish without configuring your account settings first, the Quick Publish Configuration dialog will automatically open for you to do so.

The Uploading Files dialog briefly appears before your page is displayed in your chosen browser.

Creating PDFs

WebPlus allows you to publish your entire site as a PDF and exports the site structure as clickable bookmarks within the PDF document.

> Publishing as a PDF is significantly useful for students who need to submit their site(s) in document format to examination boards.

1. Click the 📷 ▼ **Publish site** flyout on the **Standard** toolbar and select **Export site as PDF...**

   -or -

   Click **File>Publish Site>Export site as PDF...**

2. In the **Publish to PDF** dialog assign a **File name**, browse to the folder in which you want to save your PDF and click **Save.**

The PDF is generated and providing that you have a suitable PDF viewer installed on your system, will automatically open for you to view.

✎ If problems were identified during the generation of the PDF, a list of the issues will be displayed.